QUIET MOMENTS
with John Powell, S.J.

Also by John Powell

QUIET MOMENTS
with John Powell, S.J.

120 DAILY READINGS

Selected and Edited by
Nancy Sabbag

CHARIS

SERVANT PUBLICATIONS
ANN ARBOR, MICHIGAN

Charis Books is an imprint of Servant Publications especially designed to serve
Roman Catholics.

Published by Servant Publications
P.O. Box 8617
Ann Arbor, Michigan 48107

The publisher would like to thank St. Thomas More Press for permission to reprint
excerpts as noted at the back of this book. All rights are reserved by St. Thomas
More Press.

Cover design: Design Team, Grand Rapids, Michigan

00 01 02 03   10 9 8 7 6 5 4 3 2 1

Printed in the United States of America
ISBN 1-56955-218-5

LIBRARY OF CONGRESS CATALOGING-IN-PUBLICATION DATA

Powell, John Joseph, 1925-
   Quiet moments with John Powell, S.J.: 120 daily readings/selected and edited by
   Nancy Sabbag.
      p.   cm.
   Includes bibliographical references.
   ISBN 1-56955-218-5 (alk. paper)
   1. Christian life—Catholic authors. 2. Devotional Calendars—Catholic Church.
   I. Sabbag, Nancy.   II. Title.
BX2350.2.P642   2000
242'.2—dc21   00-031753

For
Joyce Lombana Aragno

"I thank God in all my remembrance of you …"

Contents

Introduction

Several years ago, I attended an adult learning conference for educators from all over the United States. As a way of warming up the audience on the first day, the speaker asked us: "How many of you get along with most people?" A scattered few in the crowd raised their hands—and so did I. It was true. I did get along with most people, and I didn't really understand why so many others indicated they didn't. I was struck when the lecturer quipped: "Those of you who raised your hands just don't know enough people." The audience erupted in laughter, but the speaker's premise—that we can expect difficulty in our relationships—was lost on me. That is, until several years later, when I began to understand a deeper truth about myself.

As a child, I had been a "people pleaser." Giving people the response or the control they wanted guaranteed relationships with little discord and less friction. Life worked well that way. I kept conflict at bay to mitigate the risk of hurt, failure, or abandonment in relationships. Pleasing people became all-important, even if it meant keeping my self submerged.

It was only later in my adulthood, after the traumatic, unexpected death of a loved one, that I began to wake up. For months after my loss, overwhelming grief sapped my energy for everything—*especially* pleasing other people. In my vulnerable "survive mode" many of my pretenses came crashing down and many of my genuine feelings—so successfully buried behind my pleaser mask—came rushing to the surface. I hardly recognized myself or my sometimes unpleasant reactions. I felt for the first time that relationships *were* difficult. And I realized I had never really gotten to know myself beyond my well-practiced role. That season following tragedy set me on an important journey of self-discovery and growth.

Why do I tell you this story to introduce *Quiet Moments With John Powell?* Because, like me, many of us hide behind well-chosen masks to preserve ourselves from life's threats and risks. Our *modus operandi* usually works well as long as everything is status quo. But what we don't realize is that the roles or "acts" we have adopted are eclipsing our real selves, keeping us from understanding and becoming all God created us to be. As Fr. John Powell puts it, they keep us from becoming "fully alive."

For more than three decades, the popular lecturer, teacher, and author has been challenging adults to reach their full potential in life by embarking on a journey of self-knowledge and continued growth. This may mean throwing off some well-established patterns and life habits, and adopting instead some new principles for living life to the fullest.

This volume, compiled from more than a dozen of John Powell's best-selling works, offers a glimmer of the author's most poignant insights on the principles of personal growth, the importance of self-acceptance, the requirements for honest relationships, the significance of service to others, the earmarks of unconditional love, and the rewards of a life of faith.

Like many at the conference that day, you may be aware of difficulties in your relationships. Like me, you may be ready to drop your role and get to know yourself better. Come along as Father Powell shows us that loving ourselves is a prerequisite to loving others; that taking responsibility for our actions, emotions, and behaviors is the first step to real self-knowledge; that for us to be all we can be, transparent and permanant relationships are necessary; and that real fulfillment comes from exercising our ability to stretch and risk in new ways every day.

A full life is waiting. Enjoy the journey.

Nancy Sabbag

Insights for a Fuller Life

"... When we shut out the world's suffering, we also shut out its joy. We have only one set of doors to the world."

John Powell, S.J., *Through the Eyes of Faith*

1. Life Asks Many Questions

...Life asks many different questions of us. Life asks how much we can love, how much we can enjoy and endure. Life asks us if we love ourselves and if we love our fellow human beings. Daily living asks us to distinguish between what is really important and what is unimportant in life: to choose priorities. Life demands that we exercise the judgment of conscience: to choose whatever seems right and to avoid whatever seems wrong. Perhaps the most profound question asked by life is the question of significance and meaning. All of us have to find some purpose or mission in life which will confer upon us a sense of personal distinction and worth. We need to believe that our lives will make a difference for someone or for something.

Of course, there are no patented, simple answers that flow out of automated machines. The German poet Rainer Maria Rilke counsels us to be patient toward all that is unsolved in our hearts. He suggests that we must learn to love the questions themselves while waiting for and working out the answers. Growth is always a gradual process even if there are glittering moments of insight and divine revelation.

2. Why Don't We Live More Fully?

Psychologists and students of human nature tell us that the average person achieves only ten percent of his or her potential to live, to learn, to love, to enjoy, and so on.

Where does the other 90 percent go? Cardinal Newman once said, "Fear not that your life shall come to an end; rather fear that it will never have a beginning."

What happens to our human potential? Why don't we live more fully? Why don't we savor every moment of this great opportunity called life? According to many psychologists, the reason we do not live up to our potential and enjoy our human life to the fullest is because of our attitudes, or vision of reality.

Each of us has a vision of reality that controls everything else about our life…. It is the way we look at ourselves, at other people, at life, at the world around us, and at God…. I would like to suggest that 95 percent of our suffering grows out of a wrong or distorted way of looking at reality….

…Consequently, if we are to change—to grow—we must first change our basic vision, our perception of reality.

3. A Way Into Fuller Living

Fully alive people are glad to be alive and to be who they are…. For such people, life has the color of joy and the sound of celebration…. Each tomorrow is a new opportunity which is eagerly anticipated. There is a reason to live and a reason to die. And when such people come to die, their hearts will be filled with gratitude for all that has been … for a beautiful and full experience.

…Fully alive people experience failure as well as success. They are open to both pain and pleasure…. They feel the strong stings of growing—of going from the old into the new—but their sleeves are always rolled up, their minds are whirring, and their hearts are ablaze. They are always moving, growing, beings-in-process, creatures of continual evolution.

How does one get this way? How do we learn to join the dance and sing the songs of life in all of its fullness? …A little contemporary wisdom … can be distilled … into five essential steps for fuller living.

…The five essential steps are these: (1) to *accept* oneself; (2) to *be* oneself; (3) to *forget* oneself in loving; (4) to *believe*; (5) to *belong*.

4. Step One: To Accept Oneself

Fully alive people accept and love themselves as they are. They do not live for the promise of some tomorrow or the potential that may someday be revealed in them. They usually feel about themselves as they are the same warm and glad emotions that you and I feel when we meet someone whom we really like and admire. Fully alive people are sensitively aware of all that is good in themselves, from the little things, like the way they smile or walk, through the natural talents they have been given, to the virtues they have worked to cultivate. When these people find imperfections and limitations in themselves, they are compassionate. They try to understand, not to condemn themselves. "Beyond a wholesome discipline," *Desiderata* says, "be gentle with yourself." The wellsprings for the fullness of life rise from within a person. And, psychologically speaking, a joyful self-acceptance, a good self-image, and a sense of self-celebration are the bedrock beginning of the fountain that rises up into the fullness of life.

5. Step Two: To Be Oneself

Fully alive people are liberated by their self-acceptance to be authentic and real. Only people who have joyfully accepted themselves can take all the risks and responsibilities of being themselves. "I gotta be me!" the song lyrics insist, but most of us get seduced into wearing masks and playing games. The old ego defense mechanisms are built up to protect us from further vulnerability. But they buffer us from reality and reduce our visibility. They diminish our capacity for living. Being ourselves has many implications. It means that we are free to have and to report our emotions, ideas, and preferences. Authentic individuals can think their own thoughts, make their own choices. They have risen above the nagging need for the approval of others. They do not sell out to anyone. Their feelings, thoughts, and choices are simply not for hire. "To thine own self be true …" is their life principle and life-style.

6. Step Three: To Forget Oneself in Loving

Having learned to accept and to be themselves, fully alive people proceed to master the art of forgetting themselves—the art of loving. They learn to go out of themselves in genuine caring and concern for others. The size of a person's world is the size of his or her heart…. Fully alive men and women escape from the dark and diminished world of egocentricity, which always has a population of one….

Being a loving person is far different from being a so-called "do-gooder." Do-gooders merely use other people as opportunities for practicing their acts of virtue, of which they keep careful count. People who love learn to move the focus of their attention and concern from themselves out to others. They care deeply about others. The difference between do-gooders and people who love is the difference between a life which is an on-stage performance and a life which is an act of love. Real love cannot be successfully imitated. Our care and concern for others must be genuine, or our love means nothing. There is no learning to live without learning to love.

7. Step Four: To Believe

Having learned to transcend purely self-directed concern, fully alive people discover "meaning" in their lives. This meaning is found in what Viktor Frankl calls "a specific vocation or mission in life." It is a matter of commitment to a person or a cause in which one can believe and to which one can be dedicated. This faith commitment shapes the lives of fully alive individuals, making all their efforts seem significant and worthwhile. Devotion to this life task raises them above the pettiness and paltriness that necessarily devour meaningless lives. When there is no such meaning in a human life, one is left almost entirely to the pursuit of sensations. One can only experiment, looking for new "kicks," new ways to break the monotony and boredom of a stagnant life. A person without meaning usually gets lost in the forest of chemically induced delusions, the alcoholic fog, the prolonged orgy, the restless eagerness to scratch without even having an itch. Human nature abhors a vacuum. We must find a cause to believe in or spend the rest of our lives compensating ourselves for failure.

8. Step Five: To Belong

The fifth and final component of the full life would no doubt be a "place called home," a sense of community. A community is a union of persons who "have in common," who share in mutuality their most precious possessions—themselves…. Fully alive people have such a sense of belonging—to their families, to their church, to the human family. There are others with whom such people feel completely comfortable and at home, with whom they experience a sense of mutual belonging. There is a place where their absence would be felt and their deaths mourned. When they are with these others, fully alive people find equal satisfaction in giving and receiving.

A contrary sense of isolation is always diminishing and destructive. It drives us into the pits of loneliness and alienation, where we can only perish. The inescapable law built into human nature is this: We are never less than individuals, but we are never merely individuals. No man is an island. Butterflies are free, but we need the heart of another as a home for our hearts. Fully alive people have the deep peace and contentment that can be experienced only in such a home.

9. The Question of Vision

...[Fully alive people's] basic question as they address themselves to life is: How can I most fully experience, enjoy, and profit from this day, this person, this challenge? People like this stand eagerly on the growing edge of life. In general they will be constructive rather than destructive in their words and actions. They will be flexible rather than rigid in their attitudes. They will be capable of constant and satisfying relationships. They will be relatively free from the physical and psychological symptoms produced by stress. They will perform well, in reasonable proportion to their talents. They will prove adaptable and confident when change is thrust upon them or when they have to make a decision that will change the course of their lives. We would all want to be like these people, and all of us can be more like them. In the last analysis, it is a question of vision. It is our perceptions that make us fragmented or whole. Health is basically an inner attitude, a life-giving vision.

10. A Fuller Capacity for Life

There is so much excitement and stimulation in the world of reality that surrounds us—the sights and the sounds, the light and the darkness, the agonies and the ecstasies of God's world. There is so much, in fact, that we are afraid of it…. So we shut out much of the reality and build a little house by the side of the road, laid back from the heavier traffic and surrounded by a hedge of small bushes. There we live a low-risk existence, with the sedations and distractions we need in order to cope with the limited part of reality we are willing to confront.

It is obvious that you and I do have a limited capacity. We cannot take in all the suffering or all the beauty of our world. No one could rightly ask us to do this. It is rather a question here of using more of the capacity that we do have. It would be a waste of our human potential if we were to paint ourselves into a small corner of life and stay huddled there, frozen by the fear of a larger world and a fuller life.

11. Happiness Limited

A line in the Talmud says: "Everyone shall be called by God to account for the legitimate pleasures which he or she failed to enjoy." Would you believe that many of us have only a diminished capacity for enjoyment? Some little demon haunts us, undermining our ability to let go and have a good time....

A possible explanation for this limitation of happiness is offered by Ernest Becker in his Pulitzer Prize-winning book, *The Denial of Death*. Becker contends that all of us have a deep fear of death because of our desire to be immortal. He also suggests we have a corresponding fear of life. We're afraid to take on reality, so we defend ourselves by reducing that reality to a small, workable size. We distrust our ability to cope with a larger world.

Most of us do this with pain and suffering. Whenever someone starts to cry, we instinctively say: "Don't cry." We're afraid to open ourselves to the vast tide of human suffering because we fear we will drown in it. But when we shut out the world's suffering, we also shut out its joy. We have only one set of doors to the world.

12. The Christian Vision

According to the vision proposed to us by Jesus, the committed Christian will not see this world as a source of temptation and be led to flee from it. The Christian believer knows that all those things which the Lord has made are good. However, while seeking and finding the goodness of God in all things, Christians will never become so wedded to this world through which they are passing that they cannot surrender it in open hands at the request of God or at the need of their neighbor. Christians will be fully alive in their senses, emotions, minds, and hearts. They will reach out to embrace life with all their powers. But always Christians will remain free, free from the domination and enslavement that results when we invert the biblical imperative, when we begin to love things and use people to gain further possession of those things. Where our treasures are, there our hearts will be. The Christian saves his or her heart for love and that love is kept for God, one's neighbor, and oneself....

So, I ask myself: "If I were ever to be arrested for being a Christian, would there be enough evidence to convict me?"

13. What Possesses Your Heart?

Philosopher Martin Buber told of a time he was preparing a talk for a convention when he heard a knock on his office door. A young man with a troubled look asked if they could talk. Buber answered that he was writing an important paper and couldn't be bothered at the moment. The young man killed himself that night. A young life filled with potential was suddenly ended, and no one ever remembered Buber's paper.

On that night, life questioned him and Buber responded that his paper was more important than the person. He said that he will always feel the remorse of that decision.

We each have a limited amount of energy to spend on people and things. If there is one imperative in the Bible concerning this subject, I think it would be this: "Give your love to the persons in your life. Don't ever let a thing—whether it be money or pleasure or power—possess your heart."

Whenever we wonder if we are going to have enough, our Lord assures us: "Make your life an act of love, and I will take care of you. I will be with you all the days of your life."

14. What My Brothers Need

I belong to a religious order, and [was asked to give a presentation with two other theologians in my own community].

[In the audience were] the men with whom I live and teach. I have given so many speeches in public I am rarely nervous. But this night I was definitely nervous.... So, while the other two theologians ... were giving their presentations before mine, I was silently praying. I asked Jesus to raise his becalming hand over me. Pour your peace into me. Help me to relax and do well.

Nothing happened. I mean nothing.... So I examined my nervousness, in consultation with the divine physician, Jesus. I heard his diagnosis, and the words I heard inside me that night have had a profound effect upon ... my life. He said:

"You are nervous because you are getting ready to give a performance. You want to impress your brothers, to make sure they realize what a "gem" they have in you. I don't want a performance. I want an act of love. Your brothers do not need you to impress them, but to love them."

In this communication, Jesus reached very deeply into my life.

15. The Credential of a Christian

Jesus our Lord left no doubt about the credential of the Christian. He said, "I give you a new commandment: love one another. As I have loved you, so you also should love one another. This is how all will know that you are my disciples, if you have love for one another" (Jn 13:34-35). Saint John reminds us in his First Epistle that it is impossible to love God whom we do not see and not love those around us whom we do see.

...We know that Christ takes as done to himself what we do to others. He accepts as given to himself our concern and kindness for others. In the daily battle, however, when our own needs are so throbbing and painful, we forget this.

The only attitude worthy of the Christian is that of Christ, who thought of others always, who gave himself until he had not another drop of blood to give. In his own words, "No one has greater love than this, to lay down one's life for his friends." This is, of course, what love asks of us, that we lay down our lives for others.

16. A Living Portrait of Love

…In every human being there is warmth, love, affection, but there is also hurt, anger, weakness. We stimulate and draw out of them one or the other. It all depends on our approach….

This was the genius of Jesus. He took people where they were and loved them into life. He reached into their deepest parts, found their goodness and showed it to them in the way he treated them. So little Zacchaeus, the gouging tax-collector, became an honest man. The prostitute, Mary Magdalene, became an honest and even a saintly woman.

I am reminded of those well-known words of Roy Croft: "I love you not only for what you are, but for what I am when I am with you. I love you not only for what you have made of yourself, but for what you are making of me. For passing over all the foolish, weak things that you can't help dimly seeing there, and for drawing out into the light all the beautiful belongings that no one else had looked quite far enough to find."

This is precisely what Jesus did for … everyone whose life he touched. He was a living portrait of love in action.

17. Moments of Insight

...In my quest for the full experience of human life, the most fulfilling and transforming moments have been moments of "insight."... Among the insights that have profoundly changed me and my life, I would have to list the following:

1. Obnoxious qualities (lying, bragging, gossiping, temper tantrums, and so forth) in myself and in others are really cries of pain and appeals for help.

2. A good self-image is the most valuable psychological possession of a human being.

3. The success or failure of human relationships is determined primarily by success or failure at communication.

4. The full and free experience and expression of all our feelings is necessary for personal peace and meaningful relationships.

5. I am not personally responsible for solving the problems of others. Attempts to do this can only keep the other persons immature and train them to be dependent on me.

6. Love must be unconditional or it is a form of manipulation. Unconditional love is the only kind of love that affirms a human being and enables that person to grow.

18. The Predictor of Success

It is important to remember that the way to success for us humans is usually paved with failures. Abraham Lincoln lost several elections before he was finally elected president. Thomas Edison experimented for two years on many materials from all over the world before he discovered a usable filament for the electric light bulb. When Marconi suggested the possibility of wireless transmission of sound (the radio), he was committed to a mental institution. But people like Lincoln, Edison, and Marconi were strongly motivated. So they didn't give up. They somehow knew that the only real failure is the one from which we learn nothing. They seemed to go on the assumption that there is no failure greater than the failure of not trying, and so they continued to try in the face of repeated failures....

...Clearly, desire and determination are the roots of all human success.

19. Problems—or Opportunities?

It has been said that our biggest opportunities will probably come into our lives disguised as problems. Problems have a way of challenging us, of calling out of us coping capacities of which we were unaware. Problems can jolt us out of our predictable routines but only to introduce us to a life of new possibilities. In the end, we probably profit more from suffering than we do from success. But I feel sure that the extent of benefits derived is determined by our habitual mind-set. We must be ready to look for and find the good in all situations in life....

...James Whistler, the painter, wanted to be a career soldier until he flunked out of West Point. He was so depressed by his failure that he took up painting as therapy. The singer Julio Iglesias wanted only to be a soccer player until he was hurt and temporarily paralyzed. A nurse brought him a guitar to help him pass the time. It almost seems that when one door is closed, another is opened.

20. A Good View

By definition, a goodfinder is one who looks for and finds what is good in him- or herself, in others, and in all situations of life. It is probably true that we usually do find whatever we are looking for. If we set ourselves to find evil, there is plenty of it to be discovered. On the other hand, if we seek to find goodness, there is also much goodness waiting for our discovery. If we look for imperfections in ourselves and in others, the search will no doubt be successful. However, if we look beyond the weak and the foolish things and seek to find the good and beautiful things that no one else had ever looked quite far enough to find, our search will be rewarded with success. It all depends upon what we are looking for. "Two men looked out from prison bars. / One saw mud and the other saw stars."

21. The Promise in Every Problem

I would like to suggest three benefits that suffering confers upon us. The first is that, if we work at developing the right attitude, suffering always deepens our trust in God....

The second blessing suffering offers is a signal that there is something wrong in our lives.... Knotted stomachs and tension headaches, for example, warn us that we are looking for something in a self-destructive way. If we didn't have physical, emotional, and social discomfort to remind us, we might go on trying to be what we can never be, to do what we can never do.

Finally, suffering gives us a sense of who we are and what life is all about. By definition, a pilgrim is a person making a journey to a holy place. Well, we are on our way to God's house, which will be our home forever. Suffering always reminds us that—like pilgrims—we are not yet home.

The dark and difficult days in our lives remind us that we must surrender to total trust in God ... and that we may not be enjoying the journey, as God wants us to, if we try to do or be what's unrealistic.

22. God Is Enough

Most of us go through life making our own plans and then asking God to make them come true instead of asking God what his plans are and asking him to enlighten us about our part in those plans. But God has sent you and me into this world to do something only we can....

To know ... the specific will of God presumes a real desire and eagerness to be and do whatever he wills. All of us experience some deep fear of this surrender to God. We are afraid of what he will ask of us, like signing a blank check and worrying about whether we will be overdrawn—whether we will have enough time, strength, and courage. We are like Jesus in the Garden, and God assures us, "I will be your enough."

23. The Lumber of Our Lives

God knew you and me before forming us in the wombs of our mothers. (See Psalms 139:13-16; Jer 1:4-5.) God knew of our days and of our nights. God knew there would be springtimes of delight and dark nights of lonely anguish, moments of human ecstasy, and other moments when we would feel very much alone and when we would wonder if there really is a God who cares. God knew that our gift of freedom would involve the possibility and fact of sin and that evil would touch your life and mine. God knew that we would at times refuse God's offer of grace....

...It is true that God gives you and me the lumber of our lives, and offers to help us build from it a cathedral of love and praise.... I will either use the lumber ... as a stepping-stone, or it will become for me a stumbling block. To use another analogy, day by day God gives me new pieces to fit into this gigantic jigsaw puzzle of my life. Some of these pieces are sharp and painful. Others are drab and colorless. Only God ... knows the beauty that is possible when all the pieces have been faithfully put into place. I will know that beauty only after I have put into place the very last piece, the piece of my dying.

The Importance of Loving Yourself

"Would you get a high place in heaven if you were judged only on how well you have loved, understood, and appreciated yourself?"

John Powell, S.J., *Through the Eyes of Faith*

24. God Wants You to Be Uniquely You

Just as no two snowflakes are identical, so each one of us is unique, an "original" by God. The package of goodness and giftedness that is you and me was never put together before and never will be again. God alone knows us as we really are. Only his judgment really matters. And he has said: "I could have made a world without you, but no world would have been complete for me without you. I could have made you different—a queen, a king, a genius. But I didn't want you to be any of these. I wanted you to be you, because it's this you I've always loved. So please don't compare yourself to anyone else. Just know you are exactly what I want you to be."

For a believer, all this is true, and we have God's own Word for it. The real challenge is to take it in, to make it a part of us....

...If you practice this genuine self-appreciation long enough, you will be a new person. You will be with someone you like twenty-four hours a day. Not much can make you unhappy. You will be more fully alive. This is the glory of God. But this glory can be achieved fully only when we fully appreciate the gift of God that is ourselves.

How is it like being you, being with you 24 hours a day?

25. Importance of Loving Yourself

It is necessary that you realize the importance of loving your-self. There has to be some kind of logical, if not chronological, priority to loving yourself. If you do not love yourself, you will be filled with pain, and this pain will keep all your attention riveted on yourself. Agony constricts our consciousness. If you do not love yourself, you cannot truly love either God or your neighbor. So you must learn to do the same things for your-self that you would do in loving others: You must acknowl-edge and affirm all that is good in you. You must gently try to understand all that is weak and limited. You must be aware of and try to fulfill your needs: physical, psychological, and spir-itual. As you learn to love yourself, you must also learn to bal-ance concern for yourself with concern for others. "Whatever you do for the least of my brothers and sisters you do for me." But remember that your success in loving will be proportion-ate to your openness in accepting the love and affirmation of God....

How open am I to accept the love and affirmation of God?

26. His Love Is a "Given"

God has assured you through his prophets and through his Son that even if a mother were to forget the child of her womb, he would never forget you. Your name is carved in the palms of his hands, inscribed indelibly in his heart….

…You do not have to change, grow, or be good in order to be loved. Rather, you are loved so that you can change, grow, and be good. Your realization of this unconditional love is extremely important. You must remember people like: Mary Magdalene, who was a "hooker"; Thomas, who was an all-star bullhead; the thief on the cross, who said what might have been his first prayer and was promised immediate paradise; Saul of Tarsus, who was hell-bent on destroying Christianity until he took that road to Damascus and found a loving Lord.

God was in Jesus, loving them, affirming them, forgiving them, encouraging them, challenging them all the way into greatness, peace, and the fullness of life.

What am I doing in order to be loved?
How willingly and readily do I
acknowledge that I am loved so that
I can change, grow, and become like
Christ and love like Christ Rather than
I have to change, grow or be good so that I can be loved?

27. Believe in Your Beauty

Remember Grimm's fairytale about Rapunzel—the story of the beautiful girl who lives with an old witch in a tower? The old witch constantly tells little Rapunzel how ugly she is. In fact, the witch insists, "You look just like me!"

Since there are no mirrors in the tower, poor Rapunzel believes it … so she remains a prisoner in the tower … a prisoner of her own ugliness.…

But, alas, one bright day Prince Charming comes riding by on his white horse just as Rapunzel is leaning out of the tower for a breath of fresh air.… After an exchange of reassuring smiles … the prince climbs up on a ladder of her hair into the tower. As the two of them gaze admiringly into each other's eyes, Rapunzel sees in the glistening eyes of her prince a clear reflection of her own face … that she really is a beauty.…

Just like Rapunzel, all of us, to some extent, are locked inside ourselves by our fears of ugliness, inferiority, and inadequacy.… We don't really believe that the Lord would pour his message, his song, his love into such a broken and leaking vessel. We need to be freed by the realization of our giftedness and our goodness and our beauty.

28. The Messages We Tell Ourselves

Low self-esteem is like a hand brake on a car. The lower the self-esteem the slower we move. Our God-given talents can't flow. We cannot move into meaningful relationships. It's so crippling that we have to ask: How do we ever get into this trap?

Well, there are messages on the tapes that play constantly in our heads, messages from significant people in our lives (low self-esteem is contagious). These messages may … tell us that we are not lovable or capable. But remember this: It isn't what they say to you that really counts. It's what you are saying to yourself.

What should you be saying to yourself?

"I am the child of God's heart, carved on the palm of his hand. He resides in my heart with great delight. I am a unique and unrepeatable image and likeness of God. There never was and never will be another me!"

Matt 3:17
"you are my beloved!"

29. What It Means to Love Oneself

To understand what it means to love oneself, let us first ask what it means to love another…. For now let us say only that love does at least these three things:

1. Love esteems and affirms the unconditional and unique value of the one loved.
2. Love acknowledges and tries to fulfill the needs of the one loved.
3. Love forgives and then forgets the failings of the one loved.

When we are asked to "love our neighbors as ourselves," the clear implication is that whatever we would do for our neighbor we would *also* and *first* do for ourselves…. You can't really love one without loving the other.

To understand how this would work in actual practice, it might help to think of those persons whom you truly love…. Do you think of yourself as gently and lovingly as you do those others…? Do you offer yourself the same kind of warmth and understanding that you offer them?

30. Self-Perception Shapes Our Lives

According to an American Indian legend, an Indian brave came upon an eagle's egg which had somehow fallen unbroken from an eagle's nest. Unable to find the nest, the brave put the egg in the nest of a prairie chicken, where it was hatched by the brooding mother hen. The fledgling eagle, looking at the other prairie chickens, did what they did. He cawed and scratched at the earth … now and then rising in a flutter a few feet above the earth.

…One day an eagle flew over the brood of prairie chickens. The now aging eagle … looked up in awed admiration as the great bird soared through the skies. "What is that?" he gasped.… One of the old prairie chickens replied, "…That is the eagle … the most magnificent of all the birds. But don't dream that you could be like that. You're like the rest of us and we are prairie chickens." And so … the eagle lived and died thinking he was a prairie chicken.

So, too, does each of us live and die. Our lives are shaped by the way we perceive ourselves. The all-important attitudes by which we perceive and evaluate ourselves tell us who we are and describe the appropriate behavior for such a person. We live and die according to our self-perception.

31. Attitudes: The Control Centers of our Lives

I am absolutely convinced that our attitudes are the control centers of our lives. They regulate our emotions, our health, our relationships, and the use of our talents.

I am also sure that all change, growth, and conversions must begin in our attitudes. If there is a change in attitude, it will affect all the aspects of our lives…. If there is no change in attitude, there is no real change at all.

What does an attitude do? When anything happens in our lives … one of our attitudes interprets, evaluates, and pronounces judgment; it also prescribes the appropriate reaction to the happening or the experience….

So you smile or you cry, but it all depends on your attitude. If you are happy, it is a good indication that you have healthy attitudes. If you are sad, sick, lonely, not realizing your potential, it is quite certain that there are one or more crippling or destructive attitudes in you.

When Jesus encountered people he constantly asked them to look at their attitudes…. He was saying something like this: "Your tyrants are inside you…. Change your outlook. Let the Truth set you free. Believe in me…."

32. The Stretch Marks of Victory

…We must act on insights if they are to become new habits of thinking that will replace our old delusions. Insights demand more than lip service…. They must be incorporated into one's life-style. No new truth is ever really learned until it is acted upon. This means some inner crinkling and crunch: stretch marks….

…Doing very often initiates a learning process. Suppose, for example, I am firmly convinced that I cannot give a speech in public or take unsatisfactory goods back to the salesperson. So what should I do? So I should swallow hard and do it! Yes, just do it. I must act against my phobias. Only in doing it will I learn that I *can* do it and thereby dispatch another delusion. Every day we should all do something that will extend us; we should win little victories over our fears that will widen the world and our lives. We will gradually learn in this way about the undreamed-of potentialities which we had all the time but never used.

33. The Road to Healthy Self-Esteem

Self-esteem is a choice. In the same way that we can decide to esteem (hold in high regard) a friend despite his or her faults, limitations, and weaknesses, we can also choose to accept and esteem ourselves. We can choose to accept our total self: our bodies, minds, mistakes, feelings or emotions, and personalities. True self-acceptance necessarily means that we must choose to accept all that we are. According to what we have learned so far, one way we can improve our self-images and increase our self-esteem is to use vision therapy, i.e., to replace any negative messages or attitudes about ourselves with healthier and more life-giving attitudes.

Another way to bring about and enjoy higher self-esteem is to practice the *Ten Requisites for Affirmation* (see following selection). These ten requisites are based on the assumption that we need to see reflected back to us from the eyes of another person: "You're beautiful!" Like the young Rapunzel in Grimm's fairy tale, we too need Prince/Princess Charmings who will reflect back to us our own individual worth, beauty, and goodness. Now it is important to point out that people do not give us worth, beauty, and goodness; they only affirm and reflect back to us that we have them.

34. The Road to Self-Esteem: Ten Requisites for Affirmation

1. Have fully and express freely all your emotions, positive and negative. Only then will you have a sense that others really know you.

2. Be yourself. Let your criteria of conduct and communication be who you really are, what you really think and feel and want.

3. Be assertive. Practice self-esteem. Insist on your right to be taken seriously and respected as a person…. Do not be a compulsive pleaser or a voluntary underdog.

4. Desist from all attempts at self-affirmation: like bragging, acquiring things to impress, competing, … name-dropping, gouging and clawing for fame or power in order to prove self.

5. Think of yourself in positive terms. Be more aware of your strengths than your weaknesses….

6. Be gentle with yourself. Be more ready to understand than to judge.

7. Do not be controlled by fears…. Act against them. Stretch!

8. Do not judge others or make assumptions about their intentions.

9. Look for what is good in others and express your appreciation.... Be a chronic affirmer.

10. Love others. Seek to find your happiness in theirs. Begin with empathy.

35. Cultivate a New Habit

Perhaps, like me, you remember the days when we "gave up" something for Lent…. We gave up things we enjoyed in order to strengthen our wills…. Then somebody reversed the flow of that stream, suggesting that we do something positive rather than "giving up" some pleasure. So we started attending Mass daily or we added some extra time for prayer in our busy lives….

But this is like a diet which someone once wisely advised against: "Never go on a diet because one day you will go off it and gain back all the weight you lost. What you have to do is to begin a new way of life." In other words: "Cultivate a new habit that will be with you the rest of your life."

Obviously, the spirit and time of Lent is ideal for this. Decide on something you'd like to do or be. Then practice that habit daily. It will soon become a part of you….

Beginning the practice of a new habit this Lent could mean a new life. Then Easter will take on a deeper, more joyful experience. And so will the rest of your life.

Change a habit and you can change life.

36. Mistake Makers

The human condition is one of weakness. That is why there are erasers on pencils. We are all mistake makers…. We human beings have to learn most things by trial and error. An old sage once said, "Try to learn from the mistakes of others. You won't live long enough to make them all yourself." Most of us take it for granted that if you haven't made a mistake, you have probably never made a discovery. Obviously, the only real mistake is the one from which you have learned nothing. Mistakes are learning experiences. So welcome to the club!…

So I must ask myself:… Have I let go of rehashing my "mistake-riddled" past? Have I let go of the feelings of embarrassment about my failures and regrets? Can I honestly and with peace say, "This is the person I used to be, the old me. It is not the person I am now, the new and present me"? Most of us do not realize that we have learned from our past mistakes and that we have outgrown some of our immaturities. Do I realize that the *old me* has taught the *new me* many things?

37. List Your Gifts

It's true we all have skeletons in our closets, blotches on our records, and weaknesses that keep coming back to haunt us. But setting out to look only for our weaknesses is the surest route to discouragement and depression....

With all my heart I believe that I need to know my blessings much more than I need to know my blemishes....

Let me ask you to start an inventory today of everything that is good about yourself. Include everything: physical qualities like curly hair or a contagious laugh; special gifts like musical talent or athletic ability; virtues like compassion and honesty; and don't forget qualities like friendliness and enthusiasm.

...Keep this list close at hand.... As you start this inventory of blessings, you're going to keep discovering more and more that you will need to record....

And one more thing—at the bottom of my list of blessings and gifts I've printed in large letters: THANK YOU, FATHER. For me, those words are the difference between a joyful humility and a blind pride.

38. Short of Perfect? Be Patient!

I remember what a great and endless consolation it was for me to find out that the often-used quotation, "Be perfect as your heavenly Father is perfect" (Mt 5:48), is really a mistranslation. The context of this quotation is the challenge of Jesus to love our enemies. The Lord points out that we must try to be worthy children of a heavenly Father, who "causes his sun to rise on bad men as well as good, and his rain to fall on the honest and dishonest alike." The challenge he extends is not to be perfect, which is impossible for us mistake makers, but to be as tolerant and loving and forgiving as our heavenly Father is!...

A healthy Christian attitude toward self acknowledges and accepts the human condition of fragility. But we always see ourselves walking through life hand in hand with the Lord, feeling glad to be who we are, knowing that he accepts and loves us as we are.

39. Jesus Makes All the Difference

The Jesus who asks to be recognizable in me isn't the perfect and all-good and all-powerful Jesus. I could never manage that. However, it is rather the Jesus who labors in me, who consoles me and supports me in my human weakness, that must shine out of me. It is the Jesus who said to Paul: "My strength will work through your weakness."

All of us carry the treasure of this loving Jesus, residing within us and working through us, in fragile vessels of clay. We cannot be expected to exhibit perfection, but we must be willing to stand up and to offer our personal testimonials to grace. You and I should want to say to the world, as best we can, by our words and our way of living, by our work and our worship: "Jesus has touched my life. By his kindness, by his encouragement, and by his challenge, Jesus has made all the difference in my life. I was blind and now I see. I was lost and now I'm found!" However, for myself I feel an inner urgency to add to this witness: "But please be patient. God is not finished with me yet."

40. Embracing Our Fragility

When Jesus enters our lives,… he assures us that he understands the human condition of weakness…. He promises to love us into the fullness of life…. His love is unconditional. It is important for us to know this.

I think that this is what Jesus means when he discusses human freedom with his contemporaries (see John 8). He equivalently tells them that they won't be free until they believe in him and his understanding mercy. When they protest they are no one's slaves, Jesus assures them that their tyrants are not outside, but inside them: the fears, the worries, the guilt they carry, the sense of inferiority, and the uneasiness they feel about the future. "Believe in me," Jesus challenges them, "then you will know the truth, and the truth will set you free."

…The hard fact is this: We are always accountable for our reactions and responses. No one else can accept this truth for us. But we can trust the Lord's mercy, reach out and embrace the truth of our fragility. The decision to accept ourselves as we are—in the human condition of our weakness—will set us free.

41. Loving Ourselves—Body, Mind, and Spirit

For years we have entrusted our bodies to physicians, our minds to psychiatrists, and our souls to theologians. But now we can no longer maintain this neat separation. Our physicians sometimes tell us that our aches and pains are not purely physical. They are psychosomatic. In other words, our pains are in our bodies, but are psychologically induced. On the other hand, our psychiatrists sometimes have to inform us that our depression results from a purely physical condition, like a chemical imbalance or vitamin deficiency. And theologians just may report that our suffering is not really a divine trial but is probably due to a distorted idea of what it means to be human....

Our happiness requires that all three of these interconnected parts be cared for. No one can be truly happy unless the needs of all three are provided.... We are talking mainly about the body and its needs for *relaxation*, *exercise*, and *nutrition*. However, because of our interconnectedness, in talking about the needs of the body, we are certainly implying a concern for the mind and spirit....

42. Causes of Stress: The Mountains or the Molecules?

The ancient Latin adage and prescription for happiness was "a healthy mind in a healthy body." … The ancients were right: a healthy body contributes greatly to a happy mind and a healthy spirit.

To be convinced of the importance of the physical, try to recall how you reacted to a given stimulus when you were relaxed. Then recall how you have reacted to the same stimulus when tense, tired, or hungry. Oftentimes it isn't the big things that cause us tension and stress. It's the snapped shoelace when you don't have time to find another. When driving, it is the turn you "can't miss." Stress and the tension it produces magnify all these small irritations of life. We usually don't trip over mountains but molecules….

The body reacts immediately to any stress, whatever its source. Overwork, the loss of a job, a death or divorce can easily cause chronic stress. But small things like a time deadline, a simple quarrel, or a gadget that doesn't work can throw us off balance. The message of "Stress!" is immediately carried along neuron, or nerve, tracks and stimulates an increased production of the chemicals of tension. The effects are almost immediate. When the body becomes tense, the functions of mind and spirit are immediately diminished.

43. Stress Signals

The first step in combating stress is to relax…. And the first step to learning how to relax is to recognize our stressors. At your first opportunity make a list of the people, the activities, the situations that tend to create stress in you. Also, most of us have what is known as the "target organ" of stress. It will help you if you can identify your target organ and attend to its signals. Some of us get headaches; others get backaches. Some are troubled by stomach upsets; others get skin rashes. When I begin to feel pressure in my sinuses, I know it is time to shift into a slower gear.

Some stressors seem to help us; others tend to diminish us. Stress in our lives has been compared to the friction of a violin bow. If there is no friction, there is also no music. If there is too much friction, there is only a painful screeching. Helpful stress gets us going. Helpful stress situations seem to excite us and energize us. I have often thought that going into a classroom to teach is a helpful stressor for me. I almost always feel stimulated by the prospect.

44. Stress Conversion

Some stressors that tend to be destructive can be converted into helpful stressors. For example, most of us find only a destructive stress in harboring resentment. We tend to judge harshly those whom we resent.... We try to conceal our resentment, but afterward we feel drained....

How do I go about converting the stress of resentment?... Something that helps me very much is the realization that in resenting another, I have put my happiness in the hands of that person. I have given that person a very real power over me. The change ... will take place at the moment I truly take back the responsibility for my own happiness. This usually means I must forgive the person I resent. I have to release that person from the real or imagined debt owed me, and I have to release myself from the high price of resentment.

45. Relaxing by Techniques

...Not all negative stressors can be converted into positive stressors. For example, the death of a dear one means that we must go through a grieving process. There is no shortcut through this sorrow.... [But] whether our tensions result from major grief or from everyday stress, we all need to practice some helpful forms of relaxation.

One common technique is to set aside some time each day for a hobby that has a pacifying, relaxing effect.... I usually play the piano and relax....

Still another popular technique is to make a daily appointment with yourself. During this appointment time, try to learn to enjoy the peace of doing nothing.... Sit back and close your eyes. Breathe deeply, all the way in and all the way out. Imagine yourself in a place of peace ... a delightful place.... Feel all your muscles unstretching. Relax and enjoy this daily appointment with yourself. It's cheaper and better than Valium.

46. Just Do It!

The traditional formula for tension is, "An overactive mind in an underactive body." Daily, vigorous (if possible) exercise restores the balance. It also releases the buildup of tension. What exercise does for us physically is clear out the brain and bloodstream of the chemicals of tension. Exercise also promotes the production and flow of the chemicals that make us feel relaxed and peaceful, like the endorphins. It is very difficult to be depressed after vigorous exercise. Joggers often experience a feeling of exhilaration, commonly called runner's high. Physically, it is a neuro-chemical change in the body brought on by exercise.

It is interesting to note what many authors [who wrote about] midlife crisis recommend above and before all: daily, vigorous exercise. Often psychological or spiritual needs assert themselves most forcibly at midlife. The result is not only the intrusion of our old friend, stress, but a vicious circle that apparently traps many of us. We get into the circle when our needs produce stress, and the quickest way out is daily, vigorous exercise. Jog, swim, walk briskly, but do something!

47. Stepping Out of Our Comfort Zones...

Each of us lives for the most part in the safe confines of a comfort zone. As long as we stay within that area, we feel secure and we know what to do....

One of our obstacles to growth is that we tend to rationalize these comfort zones.... We say, "That's just not me." "That's not my style."... The most successful rationalization is simply to say, "I just can't."

The deliberate stepping out of our comfort zones is what we mean by "stretching."... Stretching challenges us to do something that seems right and reasonable, but from which we have always been inhibited by fear....

Obviously, all growth involves some stretching. I have to attempt new things if I am to change. At first, I may feel clumsy, awkward, and more than a little self-conscious. But every time I try the same stretch, I will be a little more comfortable. Finally, what was once outside my comfort zone will now be within it. Repeated stretching will usher me into a new and larger world. I will be much more free. Eventually I will develop a "stretch mentality." I will actually enjoy trying new things.

48. ...And Stepping Into the Sun

I remember reading about the liberation of the Nazi concentration camps by the Allied Forces at the end of World War II. It seems that many of the prisoners came hesitantly out of their prison barracks, blinked in the sunlight, and then slowly walked back into those barracks. It was the only life they had known for such a long time. They were accustomed to think of themselves as prisoners. They couldn't imagine themselves as free. So they weren't able to adapt immediately to acting like free human beings. I think that all of us somehow share this very human tendency. We have been imprisoned by our fears for such a long time.... We blink in the sunlight and want to go back silently to the things we have known, to our cramped but familiar comfort zones.

...When we give up one pleasure, we must be consoled by ... a greater pleasure.... The pleasure we give up in stretching is safety.... The substitute pleasure in stretching is freedom ... slowly coming out of our darkness into the light, out of our loneliness into love, out of our partial living into the fullness of life.

49. Areas for Stretching

The possibilities for stretching are as large as the world a person wants to live in. But there are certain areas that for many of us seem to need special consideration. The first of these is *the expression of emotions.* It has been demonstrated again and again that the bottling up of our feelings inside us is self-destructive....

A profitable area for stretching could be included under the title, "Things I have always wanted to do but have been afraid to try." ...Let me include here some typical challenges: giving a speech, telling others how grateful we are, disagreeing with a teacher or a boss ... flying through the skies ... speaking up when silence would be so much easier....

Certainly included in areas for stretching would be *personal authenticity,* or *realness....* I will always, in a mature way, make known my needs. I will not be afraid to ask favors from others.... And if something hurts, I will say an audible "Ouch!" I will be honest and open and real! And I am nothing if not real.

50. 1, 2, 3–Stretch!

Try one of the following "stretches" every day…. See for yourself how these stretches will release you from the small and lonely world of comfort zones. Experience the liberation of acting against your fears and painful inhibitions. Remember: one a day, and one stretch at a time.

1. An emotion I have never shared. I will share that emotion today.

2. A risk I have never taken. Today I will take that risk.

3. An achievement I have never tried. Today I will try for that achievement.

4. A rejection I have never chanced. Today I will take that chance.

5. A need I have never admitted to anyone. Today I am going to admit that need.

6. An apology I have never been able to make. Today I will make that apology.

7. An affirmation I have never offered. Today I am going to offer that affirmation.

8. A secret I have never shared. Today I will share it with someone.

9. A hurt I have never revealed. Today I will reveal that hurt.

10. A love I have never expressed. Today I am going to tell someone "I love you."

Principles for Personal Growth

"We must be trying to learn who we really are
rather than trying to tell ourselves
who we should be."

John Powell, S.J.,
Will the Real Me Please Stand Up?

51. Entrance Into a Full Life

Our participation in the fullness of life is always proportionate to our vision. Whoever is not living fully is not seeing rightly. However, to give up an old vision in favor of a radically different perspective always involves the limbo of the in-between, the temporary existence of chaos. This is why there is always an initial period of disorientation or disintegration. It is a necessary part of the growth process.

Have you ever tried to cross a stream stepping from one rock to another? While perched on any one rock there is a sense of security. It is safe. Of course there is no movement, no progress, no satisfaction beyond safety. The challenge to move on—to step out to the next rock—is precarious and frightening precisely because of that moment when one is firmly footed on neither rock. The precarious and frightened feeling is comparable to what we feel at the moment an insight beckons and we are tempted to step out of rigidity into a new vision and into a new life....

52. The Child's Inherited Vision

A baby's first question concerns self: Who am I? The perceived answers to this question, and consequent perception of self, will be ... most important.... If children are loved and perceive themselves to be loved for themselves, they will develop a good self-image and be on their way to fulfilling lives. If they are loved for what they look like or can do for others, they are on their way to diminished lives.

The second question of children is about others. Who are they? Parents will answer this question more by example than by precept. Children watch and listen for answers. They watch the expressions on the faces of their parents and listen to the inflections of their voices as they talk to and about other people. Parental reactions are repeated; messages are reinforced; child thoughts become adult attitudes....

... The child asks [the third question]: What is life for? Who is a success and who is a failure at life?... The answer received will become an integral part of the child's first vision....

Eventually the child will be graduated from the home and family situations, but the old parental messages will continue to play softly on the CD player of the brain: "Life is...." "Success is...." "The most important thing is...."

53. Revising the Inherited Vision

Children learn who they are and what they are worth, who other people are and what they are worth. Children learn to cherish life as a beautiful opportunity or to despise it as drudgery. They discover the world is wide and warm and beautiful, or they walk along with eyes cast down through an unexamined world. It is all a matter of the vision they inherit....

Inevitably children will revise this inherited vision. Their own observations and experiences will to some extent contradict, enlarge, and modify the pictures that were drawn for them.... The key to revising and modifying one's first vision—the key to growth as a person—is openness and flexibility. Obviously, the more open and flexible a person is or becomes, the more he or she will be able to change the inherited vision....

[Our] vision of reality ... determines our emotional patterns of our lives, our physical responses, and our behavioral reactions and actions. In short, something inside of us, namely, our attitudes about self, other people, the world, and God determine all our actions and reactions.

54. What Is in Me?

The crucial insight and realization, which opens up a whole new dimension of personal growth, is this: Something in me—my attitudes, my vision of reality—determines all my actions and reactions, both emotional and behavioral. Something in me is writing the story of my life, making it sad and sorrowful or glad and peaceful. Something in me will ultimately make the venture of my life a success or failure. The sooner I acknowledge this, taking responsibility for my actions and reactions, the faster I will move toward my destiny: the fullness of life and peace....

I must not let this remain a matter of words, a lip-service admission. I must ask myself if in fact I really believe this. Am I really convinced that my inner attitudes evaluate the persons, events, and situations of my life and regulate all my reactions? If so, I must press on and ask, "Do I truly believe that it is within my power to change these attitudes, wherever necessary, in order to have a full and meaningful life?" If I am convinced on both scores, then I must close all the escape-from-reality doors and walk bravely down the corridor of personal responsibility.

55. Our Past: Prologue for the Present

Everything that has ever happened to you and to me, from our prenatal experiences on, is recorded on these very sensitive and retentive instruments known as our brains.... Some of the material stored in our brains obviously antedates our active memory, which usually begins about ages three to five. Other materials have been quietly but effectively repressed, rationalized, or simply denied out of existence. But all remain indelibly engraved on our brains and influence our actions and reactions....

What comes from us, in the form of thoughts, feelings, or actions, comes out of something that has been stored up in us. If I get angry or envious, there has to be some anger or envy already in me. And, chances are, it has been there for a very long time. If there is a lot of anger in me, it will squirt out often and in various directions....

Our past thus becomes a prologue for the present and future days of our lives.

56. What Is "Full Responsibility"?

Every one of us knows from personal experience that we are not completely free. There are times when our reactions completely escape from the reins of self-control…. So what's this about accepting "full responsibility"?…

…We have all been programmed from infancy through childhood. And this programming limits our freedom…. Habits, too, diminish our freedom to choose…. With Saint Paul we must admit, "I see the right thing, I intend to do it, and then I do just the opposite."…

Clearly, full responsibility does not imply full freedom…. What full responsibility means is this: There is *something in me* that determines my actions and responses to the various stimulations and situations of life. It may be the result of my genes, my programming, or the force of my own habits. But it is *something in me*. I take full responsibility for that. I do what I do, say what I say, because of something in me. Other persons or situations may *stimulate a response*, but the *nature of that response* will be determined by something in me.

57. Old Emotions ... New Insights

The patterns of our emotional lives are simple and tangible reflections of the patterns of our perceptual lives. Consequently, my first important effort must be a full, accurate, and conscious awareness of my emotions. I must have and acknowledge my emotions before they can guide me to the perceptions from which they have stemmed.... If I were ... [then] willing to dig for their roots, I would have easy access to the perceptions, to the vision that shapes my life.

In tracing my emotional panic [after my car broke down on a busy Chicago freeway] to its perceptual source, I made a surprising discovery. Strangely, it was not danger to life or limb that was found at the roots of my panic.... It was the fact that I was not in control of the situation.... A part of my own identity and sense of worth has somehow been attached to being in control of every situation. Once I discovered this, I was later able to relate this new awareness to other situations in my past life.... Being in control ... of every situation was part of my security operation. The elimination of this distortion is clearly one condition of my growth as a person....

58. Why Don't We Change?

Let us imagine a man with a totally distorted vision. He sees himself as a one-man slum. He regards other people as mean and menacing. Life for him is an endurance contest, the world is a snake pit, and God is little more than a cruel illusion. Obviously such a man would want to stop the world and get off. His perceptions punish him brutally. Why doesn't such a person rethink and revise his vision? He must notice that there are other people who are relatively happy…. Did they swallow some secret joy?… He could replace a negative mental attitude with one that is positive. Why doesn't he? To a lesser or greater degree we all somehow resemble this poor man.

…In every change there is a death and a rebirth. Dying to the old and being born into the new is a frightening prospect. And there is always that terrible moment between death and rebirth when I will have nothing. If I give up the old vision, which made some sense of life and provided a source of direction for my behavior, will the new vision keep my life intact the same way?

59. Defense #1: Repression

…The problem of getting to know ourselves comes from the difficulty we have with digging into the layers of ourselves. As we try to dig through these layers we are often stopped abruptly by what seems like solid granite. The common interpretation of this impasse is that we have all developed defenses which are intended to spare us from honest confrontation with ourselves.

These defenses form shields around us … to prevent us from being overwhelmed by life. However, these defenses also shield us from knowing our own inner and true selves….

The first of the three most common defenses is called REPRESSION. We are capable of hiding the truth from ourselves. We repress that truth by pushing it down into our unconscious minds….

It is important to know this much, that what we have stored in the unconscious is buried alive, not dead. These hidden things (events, feelings, reactions, prejudices) continue to haunt, to bother, and to influence us. However, just as we are not aware of the things we have hidden, we are also not aware of their impact on our thoughts, actions, and reactions. And this impact can so easily make a great difference in our daily lives.

60. Defense #2: Rationalization

The second defense we commonly use is called RATIONAL-IZATION. Rationalization usually occurs when we are in the position of choosing between good and evil…. My mind (the power to know) proposes a choice to my will (the power to choose). The will can only choose that which is of personal benefit. It can't choose evil as an evil. It has to be reaching out for something that is seen as good. My will orders my mind in this case to rationalize the evil….

In the world today, the media, our entertainment, and culture do not help us to be honest with ourselves. In fact, they help us rationalize by doing much of the work for us. They make things which at first seem wrong to us sound so right…. Societally we seem to have rationalized violence, sexual indulgence, lying, and stealing…. Our media has helped us euphemize evil. In our effort to rationalize, we cannot afford to be honest, to name things truthfully.

61. Defense #3: Denial

The third of our defenses is simply called DENIAL. We close our minds to the reality that we don't want to face. We block out a part of reality because it is emotionally painful…. Harry Stack Sullivan, the psychiatrist of interpersonal relationships, calls this denial "selective inattention." He insists that we pick out a "security operation," something like a specialty, and then simply deny the opposite. It does not fit into the picture we have chosen to see.

For example, if I pick out as my "security operation" being a humorist, I have to deny all the sadness and cruelty in life. This is my way of viewing life. I simply take the stand that "everything's coming up roses." If anyone tries to dissuade me of this in one way or another, I let them know my mind is closed. I keep repeating the thesis by which I live….

…We go on blithely believing and mouthing these lies … while the opposite reality stares at us or boils somewhere deep inside us.

62. Our Unconscious Material

One psychiatrist I know theorizes that 90 percent of our actions and reactions are governed by "unconscious material." If I resented my mother, for example, but could never acknowledge that resentment, I repress that feeling. Then, without knowing, I act it out, taking out my hidden resentment on other women who come into my life. As long as I keep the original resentment hidden or "denied," I never realize that I am displacing my anger on innocent people.

Freud, who discovered the unconscious..., said the things we have hidden in denial are like wood held under water. These repressed realities tend to surface for recognition....

An important part of the solution is to become an "owner" and not a "blamer." We have to become personally responsible for all our actions and responses to life.... We can't say things like "You make me mad ... She really drives me crazy...."

Other places, things, and persons can only stimulate what is already inside us. They cannot cause things which are not in us already. So the profitable question is always: What is in me? One of the truisms about human nature is this: "Growth begins where blaming ends."

63. "Owning" What's in Me

The starting point for all true self-knowledge is ownership. I must acquire new habits of thinking and speaking. I must acknowledge that all my actions, reactions, and feelings come from something in me. I may not always have faucet-control over these things. And I certainly do not mean to imply any moral responsibility. Still, I have to own whatever is in me. It is a part of me, however it got there. I must never place the blame at another's feet.... My behavior and my feelings are mine!... If I truly accept this, I will instinctively make "I" rather than "you" statements. I will never say, "You hurt me." Only this, "I felt hurt."

A much-needed word of caution here. I must eliminate the word "blame" from my thoughts and vocabulary. It is most important that I do not blame others for my reactions and equally important that I do not blame myself. I must presume myself innocent until proven guilty, and a guilty verdict calls for a judgment which I simply cannot make. In taking responsibility for my behaviors and feelings, I simply acknowledge that they come from something in me. It could understandably help me if I knew how this "something" got into me, but I may never know its exact source of origin.

64. Accepting Our Truth

No one else can cause or be responsible for my emotions. Of course, we feel better assigning our emotions to other people. "You made me angry … You frightened me … You made me jealous…." The fact is that you can't make me anything. You can only *stimulate* the emotions that are already in me, waiting to be activated…. The acceptance of the truth involved is critical. If I think you can make me angry, then when I become angry I simply lay the blame and pin the problem on you. I can then walk away from our encounter learning nothing. I conclude only that you were at fault because you made me angry. Then I need to ask no questions of myself….

If I accept the thesis that others can only *stimulate* emotions already latently present in me, [the experience] becomes a learning experience. I then ask myself: Why was I so afraid? Why did that remark threaten me?… Something was already in me that this incident called forth. What was it? People who really accept total responsibility will begin dealing with their emotions in a profitable way…. They will grow as they get more and more in touch with themselves.

65. Behaviors of Blamers and Owners

…If I blame my actions and feelings on someone else, I will learn nothing about myself. The unfortunate *blamer* keeps assigning responsibility to other people, other places, or other things: "You made me mad." "This place bores me."… "He made me feel so small." The poor blamer keeps repeating supposed facts. It is a classic ego-defense mechanism called projection. Once stuck here, the blamer is removed from reality. There is no possibility of growing up. The magnificence of what might have been is lost until the blamer becomes an *owner*. Growth begins where blaming ends.

The owner asks the only profitable questions: "What's in me? Why did I choose to do that or feel that way?" Notice please that the owner does not excuse or explain away obvious misconduct on the part of others. Owners may well think of the behavior of others as regrettable or even destructive. But owners know they can only change themselves….

66. An Owner or a Blamer?

…A caution about not blaming, others or myself. I can't blame others because I do not know if they actually did or said to me what my own interpreting memory tells me…. Maybe they were trying to do their best. Nor should I blame myself. Maybe it was actually as I remember it, maybe not. Why I imitated a given mannerism or interpreted something as I did is really not a fair question. I just can't know. The only fair question concerns my willingness to accept responsibility for my own behavior and emotions. I must not let the child within me remain at the steering wheel of my life. I must now take over the driving of my own bus. I must put my adult in charge of my life. Under God, I must be the master of my own fate….

Only in this way can I get to know more about my true self. Owners *do*. Blamers *do not*.

67. Locating Lost Emotions

At the risk of oversimplification, I would like to suggest that if you really want to listen to your emotions, they will speak to you. Whenever you are ready to stop telling your emotions what they should be, they will tell you what they really are....

...Do you really want to know what's buried in you?... Would you be ready to admit that some of your alleged motives for action are really phony? Could you face the fact that you are perhaps displacing emotions on innocent bystanders, blaming others for things you cannot accept in yourself?...

My own answer is that I do want the full prescription but in small doses....

...To the extent that we love, esteem, appreciate, and celebrate our reality we become more flexible with the contents of the subconscious.... To the extent that we are aware of our possession of many desirable qualities we will have the confidence to face the undesirable. So a willingness and even eagerness to know the truth is the point of departure for everyone. Only the full acceptance of the full truth can lead us to the fullness of life.

68. Ego-Defense Mechanisms

…Human nature is resourceful in the matter of self-defense….
Rather than expose a self that we imagine to be inadequate or
ugly, we instinctively build walls of isolation. This, of course,
is contrary to Robert Frost's advice: Do not build a wall until
you know what you are walling in and what you are walling
out. To the extent that we experience the scars of anxiety,
guilt, and inferiority feelings, we are tempted to wear masks,
to act out roles. We do not trust or accept ourselves enough
to be ourselves. These walls and masks are measures of self-
defense….

While it may seem to be a safer life behind these facades, it
is also a lonely life. We cease to be authentic, and as persons
we starve to death. The deepest sadness of the mask is, however, that we have cut ourselves off from all genuine and
authentic contact with the real world and other human
beings. We must remember that this world and these human
beings hold our potential maturity and fulfillment in their
hands. We must interact honestly with them. When we resort
to acting out roles or wearing masks, there is no possibility of
human and personal growth.

69. Telltale Signs

Being honest with oneself requires giving up [our] acts and roles.... But prior to the surrender must come the recognition. What is my act? It has been said that all of us carry a sign out in front of ourselves. We have composed it ourselves; it announces us. We get treated accordingly. If the sign reads "Dingbat," others do not come to us for serious conversation. And if our sign reads "Doormat," others will tend to roll right over us....

My act is the price I pay for my safety and my strokes. It is the armor that protects me from getting hurt, but it is also a barrier within myself that stunts my growth. Likewise, it is the wall between us that will prevent you from getting to know the real me. Giving up my act will take much courage. I will be taking a real risk, walking out from behind my wall. I will have to rewrite my sign: "This is the real me. What you see is what you get." Be patient with me. This will not be easy.

70. Where the Real Me Begins

We must be trying to learn who we really are rather than trying to tell ourselves who we should be. A good beginning might be to develop an increased awareness of my chosen "act" or "role." Why do I choose to wear this "mask" of mine? Why each of us chooses the act, the role, the mask we do may always remain something of a mystery. However, we should try to locate the roots of this choice. And even though this act or role may … differ during various periods of my life, there is always a "payoff" of some kind. My act or role helps me cope with reality, and attain whatever it is that I am seeking. My act gets me through life with the least amount of difficulty or vulnerability….

…Whatever it is, this act usually becomes an obstacle to self-honesty and good communication. Because my act is usually rehearsed each day … I can't easily tell where my act ends and the real me begins.

71. My Own "Helper" Act

My own act was to be a helper. I usually tried to make that clear right from the start in every relationship. "I am the helper. You are the helpee." I also bridged over into enabling: doing things for others, making decisions for them, enabling them to remain weak. I didn't challenge those who came to me to grow their own muscles, to make their own decisions, to act against their crippling fears…. Helpers actually feel good about helping others. In fact, helpers aid and abet infantile dependency, but they don't have to face this because so many people are ready to thank them for their efforts….

The tragedy is that no one ever got to know the real me, not even myself. I could not have had a true relationship because true relationships demand equality. The helper cannot allow this. It would ruin everything.

72. Habitual Behaviors

Most of us play games with others in our habitual behavior. We set up others to react to us in the way that we want them to react. For example, we may not ever grow into authentic persons because we have settled for being children, inadequate and in need. We send out our "pity signals" in the sound of our voices and in the expressions on our faces. We condition others to react very gently to us....

Others of us, who are messianic in our assumed role, insist on wanting to save others at all times. We want to be "the helper" and to make everyone else to whom we relate "the helped." Sometimes the perpetual child marries the messiah, and they make a lifelong game of it together. Since these two games mesh, things will go very well, and neither of them will ever have to grow up....

Being honest with oneself ... is no easy matter, because it involves letting one's repressed emotions rise to recognition for what they really are; it demands reporting these emotions to others.

73. Self-Knowledge Practice #1: The Inner Observer

If I develop an "inner observer" and allow life to question me, I surely will come up with some success at self-discovery. For example, my inner observer may ask me, "Why did I react in the way I did?" Or, "Was it that other person's problem or mine?" "What were the deeper reasons for my feelings in this matter?"…

…At some point, it is very necessary to talk over my opinions or judgments with another person. Inside myself, I can so easily suppress the truth, rationalize, or deny the obvious. But with another … denial is less likely. Another person can see through my defenses as I cannot.…

…It is important to put out all the pieces. I must see how they fit together. When I do, there will gradually appear the dawn of self-discovery.… Another person may supply the needed connectives.… "Did you ever think that your father or mother modeled this quality for you?" "What happened at the time in your life when you changed so much?" Questions like these demonstrate the importance of finding someone for a sharing-partner who is honest but not judgmental. The questions of a good, empathic listener may stimulate new insights.…

74. Self-Knowledge Practice #2: The "God-Box"

In some groups that I have heard about over the years, there is what they call the "God-box."… The important, implied suggestion about this box is that you don't try to shoulder all your own concerns, decisions, and worries. These are entrusted to the Higher Power of God. Each person writes out a "problem" and then ceremoniously puts it into the God-box. From that point on, it is in the hands of God.

This practice might well seem to be a "cop-out." However, I would like to quote the Jewish author, Franz Werfel, who wrote in his foreword to *The Song of Bernadette*: "For those who believe, no explanation is necessary. For those who do not believe, no explanation is possible." Before a successful "turning it all over to God" is possible, one must believe that God really does want us to be happy … [and] that God controls the circumstances of our lives….

However, we must also ask God to educate our instincts…. We must ask God to inspire us to use our own skills, to make a personal effort. We must ask God to illuminate and empower us to cooperate in our efforts at self-knowledge and growth.

The Work of Real Relationships

"Many of us worry about relationships

coming to an end....

Maybe a greater concern should be that

our relationships never have a

real beginning...."

John Powell, S.J.,
Will the Real Me Please Stand Up?

75. Relationship: What Could Be?

Somehow we sense that our lives seem to go about as well as our relationships. We are about as happy as our relationships are happy. A "human loner" is a contradiction in terms. The existence of a human in isolation from others is like a plant trying to survive without sunlight or water. No new growth can occur, and the life that does exist begins to wither and will slowly die. For us to be is to be with another or with others. The quality of our human existence is grounded in our relationships.

But for all this, human communications do not have a good track record. Many people, even many married couples, seem to be involved in relating to one another without the kind of deep mutual knowledge that is the result of good communication. Many of us settle for a truce, an accommodation rather than a real relationship.

…Many of us worry about relationships coming to an end. "Breaking up is hard to do," according to the song lyrics. Maybe a greater concern should be that our relationships never have a real beginning or enjoy true growth. Maybe we are too ready to settle for a charade, while we wonder about what could be.

76. The Main Work of a Real Relationship

It has been said that a work of art is first and foremost a *work*. Relationships work for those who work at them. Unquestionably, the main work of a real relationship is communication. Communication slowly brings about deep and clearly defined relationships, but only if we keep working at it. Like any other human accomplishment, communication is a matter of continued practice....

Most of us learned to talk in the first year or two of life. And, according to the neonatologists, we began to hear even before birth. Unfortunately, most of us think that because we learn to talk and to hear, we automatically learn to communicate. That is like saying that because I can touch the keys of a piano, I will automatically play melodious music. Good communication is not an automatic or easy achievement. Think about your own problems in understanding and in being understood. It is a fact that good communication is never really achieved until two people decide to work at it. We must learn to study and practice the difficult art of communication....

77. The Monumental Challenge of Love

The truth about love, I think, is that it is indeed a profound comfort, but it is also a monumental challenge. Love immediately challenges me to break the fixation I have with myself…. Love demands that I learn how to focus my attention on the needs of those I love. It will ask me to become a sensitive listener. At times love will insist that I postpone my own gratifications to meet the needs of those I love. The kind of communication which is the lifeblood of love will require me to get in touch with my most sensitive feelings and my most buried thoughts, and to share these in the frightening act of self-disclosure. Love will make me vulnerable. It will open me to the honest reactions of others whom I have allowed to penetrate my defenses. If I have built protective walls around my vulnerable places, love will tear them down….

…These very challenges of a true love relationship, which assault our self-centeredness, are in fact the bridge to human maturity and ultimate human fulfillment.

78. Two Essential Gifts of Love

Whatever else love may ask of us in a given case, there are two indispensable gifts that are always a part of loving…. The first … essential gift of love is always the gift of myself. If I do not give you my true and authentic self, I have given you nothing. I have given you only pretense and sham.

The second essential gift of love is the affirmation of the other person's worth. If I am to love you, somehow I must … reflect back to you my appreciation of your unique goodness and giftedness. I cannot interact with you without making some contribution, either positive or negative, to your all-important self-image. Nor can I so interact with you without taking away some increase or decrease in my own sense of personal worth. We are all like mirrors to one another. We perceive ourselves largely in the "feedback" of one another's re-actions…. I can know that I am worthwhile only in the mirror of your smiling face, only in the warm sound of your voice, and in the gentle touch of your hand. And you can understand your worth only in my face, my voice, and my touch.

79. Love Costs, Love Cures

…A great psychiatrist, Dr. Karl Menninger, liked to repeat: "Love cures. It cures those who give it and it cures those who receive it." Even the great doctors, with whom we had previous occasion to disagree, are unanimous in the praise of love and love relationships as the chief source of human maturation. When Sigmund Freud was asked for a definition of mental and emotional health, he said: "It is the capacity to work and love." Likewise, Alfred Adler said that "all human failures are the result of a lack of love." More and more psychologists are coming to esteem the capacity for intimacy. People with low capacities for love relationships are ten times more likely to be labeled psychiatrically ill. The command of Jesus that we love one another seems to be a human imperative rather than an option. The experimental evidence for the crippling effects of a loveless life is found in the office of every psychiatrist, filled with children and adults who have no awareness of their own worth, no sense of identity, who are filled with hatred and fear and tortured anxieties. Love is costly, but the alternatives are deadly.

80. Barriers to Love

All of us to some extent are enduring agonies of loneliness, frustration, and emotional and spiritual starvation. Somehow these pains are radically due to failures in love. The essential sadness of such pain is that it magnetizes the focus of our attention. Pain preoccupies us with ourselves. And self-preoccupation is an absolute obstacle to a life of love.

I once asked a psychiatrist friend of mine, "How can you teach people to love?" His answer was mildly surprising, to say the least. He answered the question by asking one of his own: "Did you ever have a toothache? Of whom were you thinking during the distress…?" His point was clear. When we are in pain, even if it be only the passing discomforts of an aching tooth, we usually think about ourselves.

The psychiatrist continued: "This is a pain-filled world in which we are living. And the pains that reside deep in the human hearts around us are much worse than toothaches. We go to bed with them at night and we wake up with them in the morning…. Most human beings are so turned in by their own pains that they cannot get enough out of themselves to love to any great extent."

81. Do We Recognize a Mask—and What's Behind It?

There is a strong human temptation to judge people only in terms of their acts or masks. It is all too rare that we are able to see through the sham and pretense of masks and find the insecure or wounded heart that is being camouflaged and is trying to protect itself from further injury. Consequently, we often lash out with the iron fists of criticism and sarcasm or we try to tear off the masks in exasperated anger. We fail to realize that masks are worn only as long as they are needed. Only the reassurance of an accepting and understanding love will lure the anxious, the guilt-ridden, and the supposedly inferior persons out from behind their defenses. It may well be that we ourselves are hiding behind such masks and walls....

Generally, we can recognize masks. We have a sense that someone is not authentic, is pretentious, and we call that person a sham.... We do not realize that in the unexposed roots of these exteriors, there is only a cry of pain. There is the need to be understood and loved into life.

82. The Lifeblood of Love

Love supposes, is, and does many things, but basically it is practiced in the act of sharing. To the extent and depth that two people are committed to each other in a love relationship, to that extent and on that level they must actively share each other's lives. Another word for sharing is *communication*, the act by which people share something or have it in common. If I communicate a secret of mine to you, we then share it, have it in common. To the extent that I communicate myself as a person to you and you communicate yourself to me, we share in common the mysteries of ourselves. Conversely, to the extent that we withdraw from each other and refuse mutual transparency, love is diminished.

In this context, communication not only is the lifeblood of love and the guarantee of its growth, but is the very essence of love in practice. Love is sharing and sharing is communication. So when we say that communication is the "secret of staying in love," what we are really saying is that the secret of staying in love is to love, to keep sharing.

83. The Problem of Fantasy

The more frequently we use exact verbal communication, the less room there is for imagined messages and consequent misunderstanding. It is when we keep our true thoughts and feelings veiled—when we play games, wear masks, and pretend certain postures—that others are left to imagine our meanings. Misunderstanding always results, usually with disastrous consequences.

Clear verbal communication spares us this unnecessary suffering of misunderstanding. More positively, it also results in deep and lasting relationships.... Paul Tournier, the Swiss physician and author, has wisely suggested what many of us believe. For a person to achieve his or her full potential there must be at least one other person with whom he or she is totally open and feels totally safe at the same time. We are social beings. We are in this together. For us to be all that we can be, deep and permanent relationships are necessary. And to accomplish such relationships effective communication is absolutely essential.

84. Two Types of Communication

I would like to introduce here a distinction, based on content, between two types of communication. The first is the communication or sharing of emotions or feelings, which I would like to call *dialogue*. The second type of communication is the sharing of thoughts, values, the making of plans or decisions together, and, in general, things of a predominantly intellectual nature. This I would like to call *discussion*. Of course, this is an arbitrary distinction ... to make a point that I think is tremendously important.

My point is this: There must be an emotional clearance (dialogue) between two involved partners in a love relationship before they can safely enter into a deliberation (discussion) about plans, choices, and values. The assumption behind this distinction and the priority given to dialogue is that the breakdown of human love and communication is always due to emotional problems. Two people in love can continue to deepen their affection for each other while holding opposite opinions in almost any area of life. These contrary intellectual persuasions do not become an obstacle to love until one or both of the parties feel emotionally threatened.

85. A Diamond Needs a Setting

…When I tell you my emotions or feelings, I am telling you who I really am. I am giving you myself. While all this is absolutely true, it might at the same time seem to be saying that you *are* your emotions. This is not true at all. You and I are much more than our emotions. We have fears, but we are more than fear. We get angry, but we are more than our angers. We have minds to know, to make decisions, to accept and absorb values. We have wills, too, the heart to love and belong, to be committed and loyal….

… My values, beliefs, and goals are more important than my feelings, but only when I tell you how I feel about my values, beliefs, and goals will you be able to perceive my uniqueness. It is true that my love is more important than my feelings, but only when I share with you the many feelings that my love stirs in me will you be able to see my love as unique and unrepeatable. The diamond is the person, but the setting that brings out and illustrates all the facets of beauty is the feelings….

86. The Place I Really Live

The most universal fear of all people is to be found out, to be known and then to be rejected.... We all know that self-revelation is risky. Misunderstanding and rejection really hit where it hurts. But more profoundly, if I admitted to myself the deepest feelings that stir in me, it is possible that I might lose the self-respect and self-appreciation that I need so desperately. It is much easier to *discuss a problem* because I can always change my mind. It is much harder to *expose a feeling* because somehow instinctively I know that I am exposing the place where I really live.... It is much easier to give you candy or a box of cigars than to give you myself in self-disclosure.... It is much easier to be busy, very busy, doing a million things for you than to sit down with you trustfully and tell you who I really am, how I really feel about you, about myself, about us, about our past, present, and future. But the fact of the matter is that I give you nothing until I give you this gift. There is no other secret to staying in love or growing in love.

87. The Art of True Dialogue

There is absolutely no place in dialogue for arguing. Dialogue is essentially an exchange of feelings and there cannot be any argument over the way a person feels. There is room for argumentation in discussion, and the couple must pass eventually from dialogue into discussion. We have to know how the other thinks, what the other prefers, so that we can make plans and decisions together. Problems requiring discussion constantly enter our lives, and we must deal with them together. However, we must be sure that dialogue is really completed before discussion begins.

...True dialogue is characterized by a sense of collaboration, not competition. If there is a sense of contest, whatever is going on isn't dialogue. Dialogue is the simple exchange of feelings without any attempt to analyze, rationalize, or assign responsibility for those feelings.... If the couple is discovering a fresh beauty and new depths of goodness in each other's person, if they have a growing feeling of getting to know each other, they are succeeding in the art of dialogue.

88. The Risk in Transparency

Anyone who has ever contemplated taking the risk of emotional transparency has also asked: Can I trust you? How far can I trust you? Will you understand or will you reject my feelings? Would you laugh at me or pity me? The usual procedure is to play swimmer, testing the temperature of the water, one toe at a time. Unfortunately, most of us decide to wait until we are sure and so never get into the healing waters of dialogue.

Waiting until we have an absolute guarantee of trust reminds me of a story I once heard…. The mother of a young boy told his friends who had invited the boy to go swimming: "I am not going to allow Michael to go into the water until he learns to swim." Obviously, the only way to learn to swim is by getting into the water. Likewise the only way one learns to trust is to trust.

89. The Essence of Love

Gabriel Marcel says that "presence and availability" are the essence of love. I must be free (available) to leave my own self and selfish concerns to go out to you in a total readiness to listen and to be concerned (presence). While I am listening to you, you become the center of my world, the focus of my attention. My availability supposes that I am not so filled with my own emotions that I cannot leave them and listen with deep empathy to you and to your feelings. Wrenching free from the narcissism of self-preoccupation, especially when my emotions are painful, is difficult. However, it is a vital necessity for true listening and true dialogue. I cannot merely appear to be interested in you and what you are saying while I am in fact distracted by many other things. I must experience and convey the reality to you that my time, my mind, and my heart are yours. There is no one more important to me in this whole world right now than you.

If I have been successful in listening, I will convey to the speaker a reassuring: "I hear you!" And the speaker's reaction will be something like this: "Thank God! Someone finally knows what it is like to be me."

90. Empathic Listening

The experience of most people would seem to indicate that there are not many really good listeners among us. When we try to share who we are, many others tend to leap in, reduce us and our sharing to a problem, and proceed to solve the problem. They volunteer to tell us what to do. At other times they may seem to question the sincerity of our communication: "You don't really mean that, do you?" Or they go off into a narrative of their own, assuring us that they have gone through the experiences in their own lives. None of these reactions is empathic listening....

The empathic listener does not judge, criticize, or direct, because in the act of empathy we leave our own positions, our perceptions, and most of all our prejudices.... We break our fixation with self by getting out of ourselves and into the other's thoughts, feelings, and life situation.

...There are no automatic decisions or fixed and final formulas when we are trying to respond to the needs of another. We might have to be tough or tender, to talk or be silent, to sit at another's side or allow that person the luxury of aloneness. Only the empathic person can master this art.

91. Facing Our Friction

The growth of real love requires a commitment of total honesty between the two partners. They must agree from the outset that negative emotions will be just as welcome in dialogue as positive emotions.... The only alternative to sharing in dialogue is somehow to "act out" these negative feelings. We can act them out on our selves (headaches, ulcers, and so forth) or on each other (in periods of silent pouting, in little games of spite, in withholding signs of affection, and the like). Or we can act them out on innocent bystanders (in yelling at our children ... and so on)....

We must be convinced that the "friction" of negative emotions is not a bad sign at all, but rather a sign of health and vitality in a relationship. The absence of tensions ... is always a bad sign: The relationship is either dead or dying. Where there is life there is always some vital tension. [Kahlil] Gibran says that we can easily forget those we have laughed with but we can never forget those with whom we have wept.

92. The Miraculous Restorer of Love

An almost magical enabler and facilitator of dialogue … is the simple request: "Will you forgive me?" The beginning of most human rifts that sabotage love and dialogue is what I have called a "wounded spirit."… We can then easily be trapped in a getting-even game, a back and forth contest. When this begins, the lines of communication are down, the relationship is bleeding, and there is great need of healing.…

What I am suggesting here is that most ailing relationships can be restored to health almost miraculously by this simple but sincere request: "Will you forgive me?" In asking the question, I am not assuming all blame. I am not deciding who was right and who was wrong. I am simply asking you to take me back into your love from which I have been separated. The acknowledged need for forgiveness is the most effective means of restoration for wounded spirits. No relationship should go on for very long without it.

93. The Bottom Line of Breakdowns

I have a friend who ... contends that whenever a relationship breaks down, under all the other things that are said and done there is always a lack of forgiveness....

When Peter asked Jesus, "How far should we go in this matter of forgiveness ... up to seven times?" Jesus tells him seventy times seven would be more like it. In other words, you just don't stop forgiving....

Only with true forgiveness can we be released from all our tensions, grudges, resentments, and thoughts of vengeance. Going over my own failures somehow makes it much easier to forgive others. Some of the things I have done and some things I should have done but failed to do remain clouded in mystery for me. "Why did I ever do that? Why did I ever say that? Why didn't I keep my promise?..."

I am reminded that in our own self-knowledge we know only the tip of the iceberg. Under the waters of our lives are many unseen influences that so easily throw us off balance. Now if this is true of you and me, it's true of all others who need our forgiveness; they may not know why they did or said whatever it was.

94. Life for a Dead Relationship

Anything that causes emotional reactions is a good topic for dialogue…. For now, look through these topics and choose those that resonate in you emotionally. Let each partner in dialogue reflect and write for ten minutes, and then spend ten minutes sharing and dialoguing on what you have written.

How Do I Feel When—

…you seem to appreciate me?… I think of how our children are turning out?… I make a mistake and you point it out?… our routines or different interests separate us?… I reflect that you love me?… we are in some form of competition, like cards or an athletic contest?… we hear "our song"?… You ask me to help you?…

Dialogue is to love what blood is to the body. When the flow of blood stops, the body dies. When dialogue stops, love dies and resentment and hatred are born. But dialogue can restore a dead relationship. Indeed this is the miracle of dialogue.

Reuel Howe, *The Miracle of Dialogue*

95. The Meaning of Love

This is the test of true love: Can we really forget ourselves? There are many counterfeit products on the market which are called love. They are in fact falsely named. We can sometimes label the gratification of our needs "love." We can even do things for others without really loving. The acid test is always the probing question of self-forgetfulness.

Can we really focus our minds on the happiness and fulfillment of others? Can we really ask not what others will do for us, but only what we can do for them? If we really want to love, then we must ask ourselves these questions....

...[Do we] practice self-forgetfulness, forgoing personal convenience and emotional satisfaction? Do [we] seek only the happiness and fulfillment of the beloved? These are not merely theoretical questions. The fact of the matter is that, for most of us, our own needs are very palpable and real to us. Consequently, it is very difficult for the seed to fall into the ground and die to itself before it can live a life of love.

96. Three Parts of Loving

It has been rightly said that there are three parts of the love we are asked to give one another. They are (1) *kindness*, (2) *encouragement*, and (3) *challenge*. Only the mind and heart of love know when each is needed by the one loved. But these three parts of love seem in general to build on one another in the order given. If I am to love you effectively, I must first of all make it clear to you that I care, that I am on your side. I am committed to be "for you." This is the message of *kindness*. Once this is established,... I must help you to use your own strength by urging you to think and choose for yourself. This is the task of *encouragement*. And finally,... I must challenge you to put your goodness and giftedness to work.... You know I believe in you and that I am sure you can do it. Now I say, "Do it. Go ahead, do it!" It is the moment of *challenge*.

And so Erich Fromm has appropriately called *loving* an *art*.... In sciences, as in recipes, there are exact measures and careful directions for procedure. Not so in love.

97. True Love is Unconditional

One of the requisites that true love must fulfill is that it be unconditional. The opposite, conditional love, is not really love. It is a barter. "I will love you as long as … until … if you…." The contract is filled with fine print, and the one to whom this conditional "love" is offered is asked to conform to all the provisions. Otherwise, the contract is null and void. Conditional love is threatening. It may be taken away for one misstep…. Of course, such "love" is a counterfeit. It never survives.

I think that a lot of the anger we see in the world is a result of this conditional love. In the end, we tend to resent someone who has "loved" us in this conditional way. We feel used. We want to protest, "You never really loved me…. You loved my pretty face as long as it was pretty. You loved my clean clothes and demanded that I keep them clean. You loved my good marks and made it clear that I was not allowed to fail. You loved my abilities. But you never loved me…."

98. A Person You Can Bump Into

Perhaps the most disturbing of all fears is that my commitment of unconditional love will somehow be a denial or surrender of my self, a sad farewell to a sense of separate identity. I fear that I will have to give up my individual interests and personal tastes. In fact, if these fears were realized, there could be no relationship of love because relationship means two....

My loving you can never be an abdication of my own self. I could possibly give my life for you out of love, but I could never deny my identity as a person. I will try to be what you need me to be, to do what you need done, to say whatever you need to hear. At the same time I am committed to an honest and open relationship. As a part of my gift of love, I will always offer my thoughts, preferences, and all my feelings, even when I think they may be unpleasant or even hurtful to your feelings....

...I promise you a person, not a piece of putty.... Be ready to find in me a person you can bump into.

99. The Strength to Do Your Best

The ideal of unconditional love was dramatized for me … by a well-known psychologist…. A troubled married couple consulted a counselor. The wife complained that her husband was loving only when she kept their house in perfect order. The man agreed that this was true, but maintained he had the right to expect a house in perfect order when he returned from a hard day's work. The wife countered: "But I need to know that he loves me whether the house is clean or not, just to have the strength to clean the house."

Real love is a gift. Real love is unconditional. There is no fine print in the contract. There is no price of admission. Simply: "I love you!"… The God I know would say to the person striving to earn or be worthy of his love: "You have it backwards. You are trying to change so that you can win my love. It just doesn't and cannot work that way. I have given you my love so that you can change…. You need to know I love you whether you do your best or not so that you will have the strength to do your best."

The Fruit of a Life of Faith

"We do not pick up 'believing' as we
would learn, for example, to play the piano.
We must be touched by the Spirit of God."

John Powell, S.J., *Fully Human, Fully Alive*

100. No Final Proof

And what is faith? Whenever we make an act of faith, we take something as true on the word of another. All love relationships somehow begin with and are built on an act of faith. If you tell me that you love me, I cannot logically prove it or disprove it.... There is no final proof. Only your word. I can take your word for it, or I can refuse to believe you.

It is something like this with God and us. God has spoken to us through the patriarchs and the prophets of the Old Testament; and he has spoken to us through his Son, Jesus. He has said many things to us, about himself, about us, our lives and our world. But the most important of all these things is the summary truth: ..."I have always loved you from eternity;..."

It is the caption under the whole life, death, and resurrection of Jesus: "This is what I mean when I say 'I love you!'" The word "gospel" means "good news." And our Gospels really bring us good news: the good news of God's eternal, unconditional love ... the good news that we have an eternal destiny. We have it all on the Word of God.

101. Faith: God's Gift

Once, at the end of a long day on the road, Jesus was sitting around a fire with his apostles. He asked them: "Who do you say that I am?" Peter, who almost always spoke first, answered: "Jesus, you are the Messiah and the Son of God."

The Lord smiled at Peter…: "You have been very blessed, Peter. Human intelligence alone could not have known this. My Father has given you this realization."…

…Human intelligence cannot come to this moment or produce this experience without a very special help from God.

…Several years ago … Tommy, the resident atheist in my Theology of Faith course, lay dying. He had [previously] asked me…"Do you think I will ever find God?" I replied: "No, Tommy, but he will find you."

His last words to me were: "We do not find God. He finds us in his own time and in his own way. Only when I opened myself in love to those around me did God come in through the door of the heart I had left open."

102. We Do Not Pick Up Believing

This vision of religious faith remains for some people a sweet but mere construct, only a pair of lovely rose-colored glasses to tint and tone down the harsh demands of reality…. The decisive factor is personal religious experience, the touch of God. One must be actively engaged with and educated by the Holy Spirit, who alone can make a person a believer. Faith is not a matter of logical reasoning or a natural acquisition. It is a matter of experience. Only God's Spirit can provide the needed religious experience. Only the touch of grace can make the Christian message more than a code of conduct and comfort for pious and plastic people.

It cannot be repeated too often that a living faith is not a human skill or acquisition. We do not pick up "believing" as we would learn, for example, to play the piano. We must be touched by the Spirit of God. The difference in one who has been touched in this way is so profound that Saint Paul calls this person a "new creation." Such a one is, as we say, a new person….

103. Our Childhood Concept of God

Our childhood concept of God and faith was, if nothing else, a child's thoughts in a child's world. God was either a sugar-daddy or a slavemaster, depending on whom one listened to. What we can't do is go on clutching to or clashing with an infantile version of God and faith. We have to challenge the accuracy and helpfulness of images of God developed in childhood.

When the ache of the question of faith is upon us, we need an open mind, one that is willing to rethink, revise, rejudge.

We have learned this necessity of openness from our contact with other human beings. We refuse to categorize friends and acquaintances or imprison them in a once-and-for-all judgment, fixed and forever. Don't we owe the same courtesy to God? First impressions are often misleading, very often distorted, and always incomplete.

104. God Is Love

God's very nature is to love. Just as every being acts always and only according to its nature, so God always and only *loves....*

An analogy or comparison may help. It is the nature of the sun to give warmth and light. Now you and I can stand under the sun and allow its warmth to make us warm. We can allow its light to fill our senses and surroundings with light. However, we can also separate ourselves from the sun, in partial ways or even completely. We can put a sun umbrella, a parasol, over our heads, or we can lock ourselves in a dark dungeon where the sun cannot possibly reach us. Whatever we do, whether we stand in the sun or separate ourselves from it, we know that the sun itself does not change. The sun does not go out....

Just so, God is love. Because we are free, we can separate ourselves from God's love. We can leave God.... But God, like the sun in our comparison, does not cease to love because we have left.... In a real sense, we can *refuse* the love of God but we can never *lose* the love of God.

105. Covenant Love

It is extremely important to realize that God's love is a covenanted and not a contractual love. In a business contract, if one party fails to meet its commitment, the second party of the contract is released from all the binding effects of that contract. For example, I promise to pay you twenty dollars to cut the grass in my yard. However, you do not cut the grass, and so I am not bound to pay you the promised twenty dollars. It is not this way in a covenant. A covenant implies a promise of unconditional love, a promise that is never canceled. A covenant promises a love that will go 100 percent of the way at all times, no matter what is the response of the beloved. Covenanted love is not earned or won by the person to whom it is given. It is always a free gift. Covenanted love walks the undemanded miles, goes far beyond the demands of justice and reciprocity. Covenanted love is never taken back or withdrawn. Covenanted love is forever.

In our human experience, there is usually very little to help us understand this kind of love. However, our great God assures us: "...I have carved your name on the palms of my hands so that I would never forget you" (Is 49:15-16).

106. God Longs for Our Return

Did you ever want to love someone, to share your life and your joy with another, but your offer was refused and your love was rejected? You always knew that the gift of love can never be forced, so you allowed the person whom you wanted to love to go out of your life, away from you. But, as that person was leaving, you called out, "If you ever want to come back, and I hope you will want to, my love will be here for you. I will be waiting for you with open arms and an open heart." This, I think, is something like God's own reaction when we choose to leave God. It is critically important that we understand that God does not stop loving us, does not become angry and vindictive, anxious to punish us in order to get even....

I am sure that this understanding of God and God's love is borne out in the parable of the Prodigal Son. Jesus tells us that the father (God) allows his son to leave, but waits patiently for the prodigal's return. In fact, he longs for the return of his son.... At the end of the parable Jesus adds that there is more joy in heaven over the one sinner who returns than over the ninety-nine who have never strayed.

107. The Touch of Faith

In my favorite miracle passage in the New Testament, Jesus is walking along with his disciples. Everyone is pushing and shoving him. Then suddenly he straightens up, and announces to his astonished disciples: "Someone just touched me with the touch of faith." "So how did you know that?" the bewildered apostles asked. He answered: "I felt my healing power go out of me."

Jesus looked down at the side of the road, and there was a little woman. She admitted that the touch was hers. She told him the story of how she had been afflicted with hemorrhages for years, how she had spent all of her money on doctors, and how she knew that if she could just touch the hem of his garment she would be cured....

I keep wondering if the condition of desperation might well release us to the power of God. I keep wondering if, when we finally decide we are nothing, and cannot make it on our own, God decides to give us grace that will enable us to make something of ourselves. Maybe some of us have to be desperate.

108. The Power of God

We often speak of lacking the "willpower" to do this or that. I recall wanting to quit smoking cigarettes. I tried everything, all the medical remedies, the psychological helps....

Then one morning, I resorted to prayer.... I poor-mouthed God, told him I wanted to give up smoking, but had no lasting success. I just didn't have the strength of will.... God said to me, "I have the strength." "OK, you've got the strength, but you have to give it to me." This was my transforming moment.... I never smoked again, nor even wanted to smoke.

When I realized what had happened, I went to the chapel, and said to the Lord, "You did it. Thank you." In reply, God said, "Oh, helping you quit smoking is one of my minor jobs. I could do even greater things through you, but you are not ready yet." I thought about this for a long time. What I have concluded … is this: I had tried to quit smoking on my own.... Yet, there was nothing I could do about it. When I finally turned to God, I came as a failure. I was ready to recognize the power of God. I knew what was meant when God said: "I have the strength."

109. New Desires in My Heart

In the days of my early fervor in the service of God after entering the seminary, I used to offer God my day upon wakening. I promised God a "perfect" day, a day of perfect love and service. In my night prayers, I could only offer the Lord my remorse. It has taken me a long time to sincerely distrust my own strength and to turn my life over to God.

Only when I was willing to admit my nothingness did God begin to make something of me. In my weakness God's strength is made manifest. But more than simply steeling my will to the challenge of costly discipleship, God has come to me in prayer and put into my will new desires. Psychologically as well as spiritually, it seems so important that we be persons of desire. I am sure that every great accomplishment in all of human history began with the birth of a desire in some human heart.

So God comes to me, in the listening, receptive moments of prayer and transfuses power into me; God rekindles my desires to be God's person....

110. Prayer Is Opening Up to God

Prayer is a conversation or communication with God. In prayer we should gradually open up more of ourselves to God. And we should get to know God better. Someone might ask: What can we say that God doesn't already know? Doesn't he know the very words we choose even before we choose them? Yes. But these questions miss the point. We don't speak to God to inform him, but to become real before him.

Speaking to God means describing ourselves as we really are. Of course, we aren't fully aware of everything that is going on in us. But the more we try to share who we really are with God, the more we will get in touch with the hidden parts of ourselves. Personal prayer has suffered because most of us read prayers or say what we think God would like to hear. The reluctant prophet Jeremiah complained to God, "You didn't make a prophet out of me. You made a fool out of me." And Job told God: "I am so miserable that I curse the day you made me." Even Jesus cried, "My God, my God, why have you forsaken me?" These are honest prayers.

III. Telling God Who I Am

I now understand and approach prayer as *communication in a relationship of love*, a *speaking* and a *listening* in truth and in trust. Speaking to God honestly is the beginning of prayer; it locates a person before God. I believe that the primary "giving" of love is the giving of oneself through self-disclosure. Without such self-disclosure there is no real giving, for it is only in that moment when we are willing to put our true selves on the line, to be taken for better or for worse, to be accepted or be rejected, that true interpersonal encounter begins. We do not begin to offer ourselves until we offer ourselves in this way, for love demands presence, not presents. All my gifts (presents) are mere motion until I have given my true self (presence) in honest self-revelation.

As in all interpersonal relationships, so in the relationship with God. I do not put myself into God's hands or confront the divine freedom of choice to accept me or reject me, to love me or to loathe me, until I have told God who I am. Only then can I ask: Will you have me? Will you let me be yours? Will you be mine?

112. Putting Myself on the Line

Martin Luther's first law of successful prayer is: *Don't lie to God!* In speaking to God in the dialogue of prayer we must reveal our true and naked selves. We must tell God the truth of our thoughts, desires, and feelings, whatever they may be. They may not be what I would like them to be, but they are not right or wrong, true or false. They are me.

…Praying to God this way, exposing my raw and naked feelings,… has freed me from the lie of those prefabricated pious clichés that are death to true conversational prayer. I have told God where I really live, in belief and unbelief. I have told of my weariness in answering God's call, of my emotional resentment at being a public utility, a servant to be taken for granted. I have ventilated all my neurotic, throbbing emotions, never claiming to have *the* truth, but always willing to tell *my* truth….

There is something so healing about "letting it all hang out" with God…. So I have put myself on the line the way I am. Charades with God is wasted time. I have put myself in the posture of trusting God's greatness and understanding. This is the essential beginning of prayer.

113. A Tug on the Kite String

There is a story I once heard which seems to describe "religious experience" very well. It is a story of a small boy, flying a kite. The kite is surrounded and hidden by a low-flying cloud. A man comes along and says to the boy..., "Hey kid, what are you doing with that string in your hand?" The boy replies, "I'm flying my kite." The man looks up and says, "I don't see a kite up there." And the boy responds, "I don't either, but I know that there is a kite up there. I feel tugs on the kite string."

I remember a young woman [who nursed her mother through Alzheimer's disease for two years]. She said that, "With Alzheimer's you never know when people are going to die. However, before my mother died I went to a bank. As I was waiting in line, an enormous peace came over me. I looked at the clock on the bank wall. A quarter to two. The time seemed meaningless.... When I returned home, the paramedics were outside my house.... They told me my mother had died. 'At what time?' I asked. Then they told me, 'A quarter to two.'"

Tugs on the kite string.

114. An Instinct for God

Whenever anything happens in my own life, I wonder what God is saying. I recently sat with a chaplain in a hospital. I asked him if God wasn't saying something, perhaps several things, through the spread of AIDS? He responded, "Oh no, I would never say this."

And yet, when one closes this door, [he closes] down the question. Maybe God is saying this: "Be compassionate." Whatever the message, it is my opinion that God is saying something. As my own life unfolds, especially in major events, I wonder what God is saying through these happenings. How is God dealing with my mind and heart? As we listen and try to understand what God is saying, each of us will gradually develop a type of habitual awareness, an instinct for God. This is what I meant when earlier I wrote that faith is like putting on a new pair of glasses. Things look very different. We must learn to see through the eyes of faith. We must learn to discern patiently how God is at work in a situation. It is an acquired grace. We have to learn to listen to what God is saying. This, I think, is very important.

115. The Charity Test

I have written and given sermons on love and charity…. But it was the old problem of talking a better game than I was living. There was a painful distance between the word-level and the life-style of my existence. People were making irritating demands upon my time, bleeding me of my energies, leaving me less and less to call my own. I remember gazing at the telephone and thinking of it as an instrument of torture. It just kept ringing and those who called always had requests of one kind or another…. Weren't there some other Messiahs around…?

But, ah, the fault, dear Brutus, is not with our stars or the endless needs of humanity. The real rub is within ourselves. The basic question is: Do you really want to love? Are you willing to be the "public utility,"… there for all to use? Do you really want to let Jesus be reincarnated in your humanity? Jesus is the "man for others." If you give yourself to him, he will immediately put you in the service of others in one way or another. Do you really want to volunteer for this life of loving? You can't do it on your own. He must do it in you. Will you have enough faith to release his power into your life?

116. A God With Skin

There is a well-circulated story about a child wanting to be held by his mother at bedtime. When the mother reminded her little boy that the arms of God would be around him all night, the child replied, "I know, but tonight I need a God with skin on." There is something profound, I think, in the child's reply. There are times when all of us need a God with skin on. Everything that we know in our minds must somehow come through the channels of our senses. Our senses are the organs of our contact with the external world. So, if God is going to come to us through the normal channels of our knowing, he too must somehow enter through our senses. Somehow, God must allow himself to be seen, heard, and touched....

And this is why God has willed to fashion as his instrument a community of love which we call the Church.... Paul exclaims that this is God's plan: *Christ is in us!* (See Colossians 1:27.) God's plan is that Jesus would live on in you and in me and in all the members of his Body, the Church. God would indeed be for all humans in all ages "a God with skin."

117. Follow His Example

Saint Francis of Assisi … details some of the paradoxes posed by Jesus. Among them he says that "it is in giving that we receive."

Just think of the Last Supper when Jesus was about to wash the feet of the apostles. "Oh, no. You're not going to wash my feet," protested Peter. "You shouldn't be washing our feet."

But our Lord replied, "If I don't, you can't be my partner in the Kingdom."

The Kingdom of God, Jesus was saying, requires us to make our lives an act of giving, of service. "If you don't understand this," Jesus said, "you don't understand me. And if you don't understand me, you can't be my partner in the Kingdom."

Poor Peter, who almost always had footprints around his mouth, then invites Jesus to wash his hands and head, too!

Afterwards, Jesus says: "Now you call me 'Master' and 'Lord,' but I have been trying to give you an example to follow. You should do this for others, and if you do, you will be very happy."

This truth, like many other truths, has to be experienced before it can be believed. Like the color green. Like the taste of chocolate.

118. The Question in Suffering

Suffering is a gift which no one wants. Very few of the saints among us ask for suffering. Yet when it comes into our lives, we do ask questions which we had never asked before. It is possible to think that because we have faith this God-given knowledge answers all questions. But this does not seem true in the extremes of pain and suffering. In actuality, we grow in faith to meet these new challenges. I suppose that this is one of God's reasons for allowing us to suffer: to grow in faith. We trust that the goodness and love of God for us are operating for our benefit, precisely through our suffering.

In other words, God is asking through suffering: How much, how deeply, do you really believe? The ultimate challenge to faith, of course, is death. When death comes to each of us, as indeed it will, we will be asked: "Do you really believe? Do you really believe in an after-life, that I have a destiny for you? Do you really believe that I love you?"

119. Enjoy the Journey on Your Way Home

God says: By all means join in the dance and sing the songs of a full life. At the same time, remember that you are a pilgrim. You are on your way to an eternal home which I have prepared for you. Eternal life has already begun in you but it is not perfectly completed. There are still inevitable sufferings. But remember that the sufferings of this present stage of your life are nothing compared to the glory that you will see revealed in you someday. Eye has not ever seen, nor ear ever heard, nor has the mind ever imagined the joy prepared for you because you have opened yourself to the gift of my love. On your way to our eternal home, enjoy the journey. Let your happiness be double, in the joyful possession of what you have and in the eager anticipation of what will be. Say a resounding "Yes!" to life and to love at all times. Someday you will come up into my mountain, and then for you all the clocks and calendars will have finished their counting. Together with my children, you will be mine and I will be yours forever.

120. Look Up!

In him was life,
And the life was the light of the world.
And the light shineth in the darkness of the world,
And the darkness did not comprehend it....
He was in the world,
And the world was made by him,
And the world knew him not.

JOHN 1:4-5, 10

Dear soldier in Bosnia, look up from the guns you have
    leveled at your enemy.
People at the bar, give your minds and hearts a chance.
Dear woman, look up from your computer.
Mr. Diplomat, there is a far more important decision to be
    made.
Look up, Paris, Israel, Russia, Tokyo.
Listen again, pilot, to the voices inside.
There is a stranger at your door.

There is an all-important question to be answered; human destiny rides tremulously upon your answer.

Eternal destiny....

Dear reader, look up!

There is a stranger at your door.

In him is life; the life that can be the light of your world.

He is the Way, the Truth, and the Life.

There is a question to be answered. Look up.

Sources

Selections 103, 107, 108, 113, 114, and 118 are from John Powell, S.J. *The Challenge of Faith*. Allen, Texas: Thomas More, 1998.

Selections 10, 12, 30, 38, 39, 78, 90, and 116 are from John Powell, S.J. *The Christian Vision: The Truth That Sets Us Free*. Allen, Texas: Thomas More, 1984.

Selections 1, 3, 4, 5, 6, 7, 8, 9, 17, 25, 26, 32, 51, 57, 58, 99, 102, and 119 are from John Powell, S.J. *Fully Human, Fully Alive*. Allen, Texas: Thomas More, 1976.

Selections 36, 41, 42, 43, 44, 45, 46, 47, 48, 49, 50, 56, 65, 96, and 97 are from John Powell, S.J. *Happiness Is an Inside Job*. Valencia, California: Tabor Publishing, 1989.

Selections 29, 64, 67, 82, 84, 85, 86, 87, 88, 89, 91, 92, and 94 are from John Powell, S.J. *The Secret of Staying in Love: Loving Relationships Through Communication*. Allen, Texas: Thomas More, 1974.

Selections 55, 59, 60, 61, 63, 66, 73, and 74 are from John Powell, S.J. *Solving the Riddle of Self: The Search for Self-Discovery*. Allen, Texas: Thomas More, 1995.

Selection 120 is from John Powell, S.J. *A Stranger at Your Door*. Ann Arbor, Michigan: Servant Publications, 1996.

Selections 11, 13, 16, 21, 22, 24, 27, 28, 31, 35, 37, 40, 62, 93, 100, 101, 110, and 117 are from John Powell, S.J. *Through the Eyes of Faith*. Allen, Texas: Thomas More, 1992.

Selections 14, 109, 111, 112, and 115 are from John Powell, S.J. *Touched by God*. Allen, Texas. Thomas More, 1974.

Selections 77, 79, and 98 are from John Powell, S.J. *Unconditional Love: Love Without Limits*. Allen, Texas: Thomas More, 1978.

Selections 15, 68, 80, and 95 are from John Powell, S.J. *Why Am I Afraid to Love? Overcoming Rejection and Indifference*. Allen, Texas: Thomas More, 1998.

Selections 72 and 81 are from John Powell, S.J. *Why Am I Afraid to Tell You Who I Am? Insights for Personal Growth*. Allen, Texas: Thomas More, 1998.

Selections 18, 69, 70, 71, 75, 76, and 83 are from John Powell, S.J. *Will the Real Me Please Stand Up? 25 Guidelines for Good Communication*. Allen, Texas: Thomas More, 1985.

Selections 2, 19, 20, 23, 33, 34, 52, 53, 54, 104, 105, and 106 are from John Powell, S.J., with Michael H. Heney. *A Life-Giving Vision: How to Be a Christian in Today's World*. Allen, Texas: Thomas More, 1995.

how good am I at steering my own boat instead of being good at going with the flow